Awesome
CROSSWORDS
to Keep
You Sharp

Edited by
Charles Preston
Crossword Editor Emeritus
of *USA Today*

AARP BOOKS

STERLING

AARP Books include a wide range of titles on
health, personal finance, lifestyle, and other
subjects to enrich the lives of 50+ Americans.

For more information, go to www.aarp.org/books

AARP, established in 1958, is a nonprofit organization with
more than 35 million members age 50 and older. The views
expressed herein do not necessarily represent the policies of
AARP and should not be construed as endorsements.

The AARP name and logo are registered trademarks of AARP,
used under license to Sterling Publishing Co., Inc.

8   10   9   7

Published by Sterling Publishing Co., Inc.
387 Park Avenue South, New York, NY 10016
© 2004 by Charles Preston
Distributed in Canada by Sterling Publishing
℅ Canadian Manda Group, 165 Dufferin Street
Toronto, Ontario, Canada M6K 3H6
Distributed in the United Kingdom by GMC Distribution Services
Castle Place, 166 High Street, Lewes, East Sussex, England BN7 1XU
Distributed in Australia by Capricorn Link (Australia) Pty. Ltd.
P.O. Box 704, Windsor, NSW 2756, Australia

Manufactured in China
All rights reserved

Sterling ISBN-13: 978-1-4027-1735-2
Sterling ISBN-10: 1-4027-1735-0

For information about custom editions, special sales, premium and
corporate purchases, please contact Sterling Special Sales
Department at 800-805-5489 or specialsales@sterlingpub.com.

CONTENTS

INTRODUCTION

Welcome to the inaugural edition of our new series, *Crosswords to Keep You Sharp*. This volume is titled "Awesome" because we intend it to deliver awe-inspiring entertainment and edification: Not only will you find these puzzles fun, but you are likely to pick up some useful information along the way.

According to the Dana Alliance for Brain Initiatives, mental exercise is a key component of cognitive fitness. "Pursuing activities that are intellectually stimulating," the alliance reported in its 2001 brochure *Staying Sharp: Memory Loss and Aging*, can "strengthen brain cell networks and help preserve mental functions." And when it comes to stimulating the intellect, my 45 years as a cruciverbal editor tell me, few options are more fun than crosswords.

So whether you're an AARP member looking to tone up your mental fitness or a teenager who just wants to test your word smarts, here are 50 awesome puzzles to boggle your brain. As our expert puzzle writers themselves say at the start of a timed competition, "Ready ... set ... solve!"

—Charles Preston
Crossword Editor Emeritus of *USA Today*

1

Down and Up

ACROSS

1 Frown
6 Kind of feeling?
10 Ultimate goal
13 Western resort lake
14 Film director Clair
15 Arm bone
16 Undecided
18 Criticizes harshly
19 ___ gratias
20 Derby
21 Sightseer
23 ___ Moines
24 Part of A.D.
25 Mexican money
28 Watering place
31 Actress Geraldine
34 "There oughta be ___!"
35 "The ___ Ranger"
37 Wipe out
39 Famed song of 1889
42 Asparagus stalk
43 Kind of record, for short
44 S-shaped curve
45 Sea eagle
46 Tree's fluid
47 Secondhand
48 1920s art movement
51 Office-holders
53 Cancels
56 Tiny
57 "Mighty ___ a Rose"
60 Baseball family name
61 Topsy-turvy
64 Move nimbly
65 Passing grades
66 Keaton of films
67 Small boy
68 Ending for defer or refer
69 Be aware of

DOWN

1 ___ poker
2 Sleeveless garment
3 Buckeye State
4 Hit the jackpot
5 Hades' river
6 Writer Harte
7 Meadow
8 Writer Loos
9 Marsh bird
10 Jai ___
11 Caravansaries
12 Vertical spar
15 Extremely funny
17 Argument
22 Loosen
23 Destitute
25 Writing tablets
26 Marry in haste
27 Carpenter, at times
29 Body of water
30 Feeds the kitty
32 Criminal groups
33 Ms. Lauder
36 Jane Austen novel
38 Ogled
40 Inflict
41 Aped
49 Tennis score
50 Western ski resort
52 Wants
53 Huck Finn's transport
54 Actress Raines
55 Nullify
56 Prudent
57 Bank's offering
58 Grass bristles
59 Limb joint
62 Brief moment: Abbr.
63 Stamping device

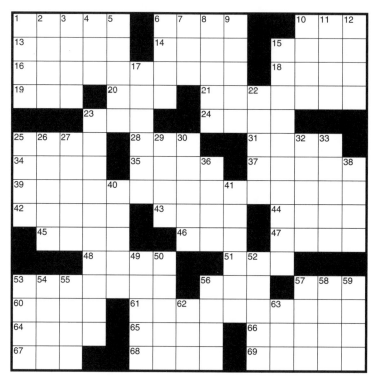

ANSWER, PAGE 56

6

2

In Style

ACROSS

1 "___ Price Glory?"
5 French monarch
10 Turkish title
14 Subordinate
15 Bird's "thumb"
16 Caspian feeder
17 Venetian thoroughfare
19 Common vetch
20 Downing or Fleet
21 Pertaining to sundials
23 Chow or lo follower
25 Exigency
26 Golfer Woods
29 Ms. Arden
32 Concede
35 Antler
36 Smiled warmly
38 Pindaric ___
39 Pre-med subj.
40 Infer
41 Dagger
42 Carry the day
43 Credit-union employee
44 Dutch comestible
45 Maugham's Thompson
47 French palindrome
48 Isle of Man natives
49 Gardener, at times
51 Barbecue side dish
53 Forest sound
57 Debt
61 Piedmont commune
62 Noted fishing grounds
64 At that moment
65 Macabre
66 LI times IV
67 Narrative
68 Takes five
69 Former HUD Secretary

DOWN

1 Jokers
2 Trumpeter Al
3 Between Shebat and Nisan
4 Flat
5 Desert plants
6 "___ bonne heure": "well done!"
7 Sleigh
8 Verve
9 Ogee molding
10 Traveled by car
11 Fashionable society
12 Mata ___
13 Actor McCowen
18 Sambar
22 Hoover Dam's lake
24 Heckle
26 Melts
27 City east of Grand Rapids, MI
28 1932 Oscar winner
30 Bank room
31 Game-show hosts
33 Paragon
34 Pours
36 Drone
37 Ending for auction or mountain
41 Alga
43 High-schooler
46 Jimmy Hatlo's "Little ___"
48 Attire
50 Toon rabbit
52 Takes on cargo
53 Steam-engine pioneer
54 Job-safety org.
55 Arboretum exhibit
56 Corn servings
58 Ending for confer or depend
59 Actor Tamiroff
60 Invitation letters
63 Insect egg

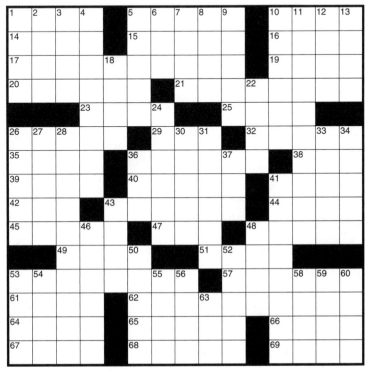

ANSWER, PAGE 58

3

Disarming

ACROSS

1 Mississippi flatboats
5 Toy-pistol ammo
9 "___ girl!"
13 Force
14 "Kate & ___"
16 G.B. or Irwin
17 "Happy Birthday" writer
18 Town and country are two
19 Phone preceder
20 Gunless Tuchman book
23 Distant
24 Land east of Eden
25 One of a packed group
27 Actor Robert and kin
31 Companion of yin
32 Ump's counterpart
33 Gunless Kipling character
35 Yokel
38 Sothern namesakes
40 Remotes
42 Celebrity
43 Sports info
45 Gunless TV western
47 Hot time, in Paree
48 Nullify
50 Leather workers
52 Bordeaux wines
55 Household member
56 "Get ___!"
57 Gunless Ladd film
63 Over
65 A Kennedy
66 March time
67 Mystical poem
68 ___ Janeiro
69 Jailbirds
70 Candid
71 Bootleggers' nemesis
72 Blackthorn

DOWN

1 Mine entrance
2 Aper Little
3 Word with jerk or bend
4 Mighty
5 ___ bacon
6 Baseball family name
7 Favorable mention
8 Curve
9 Doctrine
10 Gunless Peck movie
11 Françoise of literature
12 Hip
15 Pope product
21 Verne's Phileas
22 Salver
26 Nucleic acids: Abbr.
27 Fast time
28 Gunless Niven flick, with "The"
29 Thirst quenchers
30 Giants' q.b.
32 Naval VIP's
34 Recess
36 Feedbag contents
37 Mine find
39 Old or young chaser
41 Aids for slalom lovers
44 Printer's term
46 Perpetually
49 Tryon's book, with "The"
51 Moral principles
52 Spanish bombshell
53 Surcease
54 Passive protest
58 "If the ___ fits ..."
59 G-men
60 Billy of rock-and-roll
61 Porter's Sweeney
62 Being
64 Porky's pad

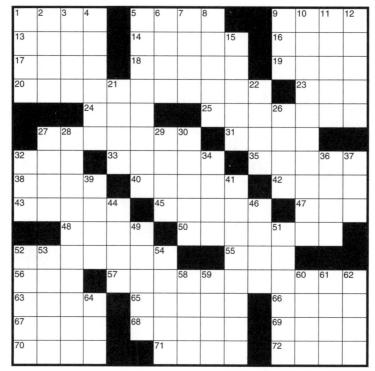

ANSWER, PAGE 60

4

Alliteration

ACROSS

1 Labor
5 Attention-getter
9 Walesa of Poland
13 Open
14 Nurse Barton
15 "Now ___ me down ..."
16 Dixon/Henderson tune of 1926
19 Logging tool
20 God of war
21 Martial art
22 Some Feds
23 Pocket bread
24 Colorful cotton
27 British composer
28 Certain degrees
31 Pizza topping
32 Inter ___
33 German philosopher
34 Shirley Temple film
37 Vittles
38 Cheers from Charo
39 Ex-Attorney General Edwin
40 Monopoly buys: Abbr.
41 In a bit
42 Showed mercy toward
43 Was acquainted with
44 Mark on a bill
45 Lectures
48 Forbids
49 Actor Wallach
52 Weather report
55 Taj Mahal site
56 Covered with fungi
57 Spanish ayes
58 Diluted
59 Madame Bovary
60 Rock projection

DOWN

1 One of the horns
2 Semiprecious stone
3 ___ fixe
4 Tennis shot
5 Veep Barkley
6 Dutch painter
7 Time
8 Kind of coat or boat
9 Sign of the zodiac
10 Essayist Lamb
11 Uncovered wagon
12 London park
14 Goddess of agriculture
17 Former Saudi oil minister
18 Singer Smith
22 Develops
23 Snoops
24 Summer noise-maker
25 Lend ___: listen
26 Cuts down on calories
27 Foreign
28 Man in a tub
29 Liqueur flavoring
30 Fine horse
32 Permit
33 Prepare dough
35 Kind of pine
36 Rascally
41 Egyptian cross
42 Duncan or Dennis
43 River craft
44 Zoo favorite
45 British dramatist
46 Senate gofer
47 He follows Ruth
48 Soothing lotion
49 Kuwait VIP
50 Eva, on "Green Acres"
51 "___ Rock and Roll Music"
53 Hulce of "Amadeus"
54 LA campus

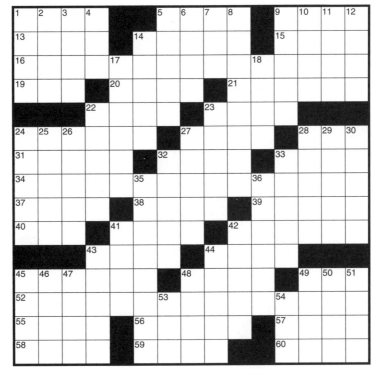

ANSWER, PAGE 62

5

Music Man

ACROSS
1 Tiff
5 Stylish
9 "Puttin' ___ Ritz": Berlin tune
14 Opera highlight
15 Mound
16 Songbird Day
17 Berlin hit
20 An Astaire
21 Pierre's friend
22 Take to the slopes
23 Greek mountain
26 Garfield's canine pal
29 Berlin favorite
35 Wearing shoes
36 Before: Poetic
37 Oak-to-be

38 Moon vehicle, for short
39 Corridor
42 Three: Prefix
43 Lend ___
45 A source of wool
46 Ship
47 "The ___": Berlin song
51 Shake-spearean king
52 Oz pooch
53 "The A-Team" star
56 Bambi's mom, e.g.
58 Real go-getter
62 Berlin duet
67 Wall painting

68 Nab
69 Shield
70 Gossipy woman
71 Avoid
72 Blockhead

DOWN
1 Continuing story
2 Urge
3 Assistant
4 Newspaper
5 Guevara
6 That fellow's
7 Ingrid, in "Casablanca"
8 Din
9 "___ to Billy Joe"
10 Neither's partner

11 Baseball's Speaker
12 Bumpkin
13 Actor Morales
18 "___ we forget ..."
19 Skirt style
24 Fortune-teller
25 Land parcel
27 Words to an old chap
28 And so forth
29 "___ was a lad ..."
30 Reggie specialty
31 Courage
32 Engine
33 Impressive display
34 Fit of pique

35 Smelting refuse
39 Comic Johnson
40 Stay behind
41 Bullets and such
44 "___ by Myself": Berlin tune
46 Like some steaks
48 Pilgrimage to Mecca
49 In the vicinity
50 Envelope abbreviation
53 "Well, well!"
54 Lewd rascal
55 Pivot
57 Jacob's twin
59 ___ girl
60 Sinful
61 Take five
63 Large rodent
64 Guido's note
65 Eye ailment
66 Sort

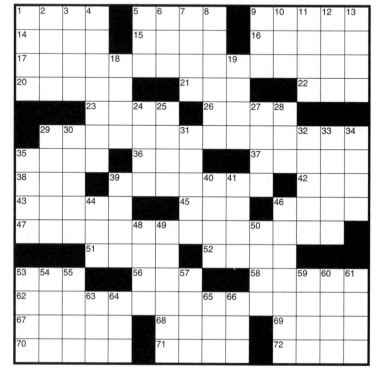

ANSWER, PAGE 64

6

Native Places

ACROSS
1 Topnotchers
5 Billiard shot
10 Bulblet
14 Patsy
15 Musical key
16 Environs
17 Thereabouts
18 Atlantan
20 Table scrap
21 Sourness
22 Impoverished
23 Fails to
25 Bridge hand, in Turin
27 Leaf part
28 Outside
32 Cher's ex
33 Lance
34 WWII outfit
35 Long, slow journey
36 Pixie
37 Mild cussword
38 Poetic word
39 Fine
40 French pronoun
41 Puts back
43 Strength
44 Flagmaker
45 Makes up for
47 Massenet opera
50 Ponder
51 Ad ___
52 San Franciscans
55 ___ account
56 Mountain: Prefix
57 Latin hours
58 European
59 Connery
60 Agora coins
61 Gaelic

DOWN
1 ___ man is hard to find
2 Large, noisy gathering
3 New Yorkers
4 Okay, in Ostia
5 Navy's goat, e.g.
6 Walking
7 Traducement
8 Mat. time
9 Ordinal ending
10 Life-work
11 Caen's river
12 Clarinet, e.g.
13 Astor or Poppins
19 Inscribe
21 Noun ending
24 Went under
25 Put forth
26 Delay
28 Heroic works
29 Alaskan
30 Flats
31 Behind
32 Ending for gang or mob
33 Mall events
36 Mink and sable
37 Venetian VIP
39 Deer's large cousin
40 Part of q.v.
42 Satellite of Neptune
43 Clutters
45 Rustic
46 Thwacked
47 Couples
48 This place
49 On the blue
50 Food fish
53 Greek letter
54 Cranium
55 Corrida kudo

ANSWER, PAGE 56

7

Encompassed

ACROSS

1 Induce
6 Gaelic
10 Hardy girl
14 French chemist: 1728–1804
15 Trot
16 Solemn pledge
17 Iran-Contra figure
19 European capital
20 Aquarium fish
21 Make do, with "out"
22 Kind of hold
23 Baden Baden, for one
25 Egyptian dry measure
28 Sheep
31 In the past
33 Clumsy
36 Hot spot
37 Turner
39 Detritus
40 In a gloomy manner
43 "... ___ death do us part"
44 Profits
45 Window part
46 Inert
47 Mexican aunt
48 Alfonso's queen
49 Bird pads
52 Government org.
54 Young boy
56 Pass receiver
58 CPA's joy
62 Essayist
64 Seoul milieu
67 So be it
68 Ash, e.g.
69 Violinist Mischa
70 Abstain from food
71 Bristle
72 Exhausted

DOWN

1 Nigerian native
2 Beer ingredient
3 Whine
4 Give forth
5 Ogles
6 Self
7 Unusual
8 Alaska city
9 Gas
10 Also
11 Wall-crumbling area
12 French city
13 Auto tire: Slang
18 Flame-thrower's juice
24 "Play It ___, Sam"
26 Record
27 Enclose
28 Occurrence
29 Caribbean cluster
30 Store green fodder
32 Start
34 Alexander the Great's birthplace
35 Linden tree: Var.
36 Literary work
38 "Toys in the ___"
41 Misfortunes
42 Prophet
50 Exams
51 Nocturnal music
53 Awry
54 Maple or new
55 ___ mater
57 Combo of two
59 Found underfoot
60 Bombeck
61 Rip
63 Picnic pest
65 Social
66 "___ luck?"

ANSWER, PAGE 58

8

Compute

ACROSS

1 Modern converting device
6 King of Norway
10 Pool frame
14 Believe
15 Computer food?
16 Small case
17 Ornamental vessels
18 Computer keyboard artists
20 Fraternal order member
21 Patriotic org.
23 Inclines
24 Defeat decisively
26 Milk containers
28 Fumble
29 Output beneficiaries
33 Computer part
34 Guiding strip
36 He escaped from Sodom
37 Refuge
39 Once-generic pronoun
40 Oleoresin used in ink
42 French donkey
43 Thomas Stearns and George
46 Cake decorator
47 Computer code
49 Milk: Prefix
51 Jaw
52 Roman road
53 "Don Carlos" and "Don Pasquale"
56 Kind of shot, for short
57 Govt. bureau
60 Character eliminator
63 "___ Get Your Gun"
65 Roy's wife
66 Goddess of victory
67 Furnishes with overhead inside lining
68 Kenton from Kansas
69 Went over 65 m.p.h.
70 Horses' ankles

DOWN

1 Stir
2 Gemstone
3 Some are hard
4 Wind dir.
5 Make a boo-boo
6 Scent
7 Useful at buffets
8 Consumed
9 On the ___
10 Mix greens again
11 Upon
12 Parish priest
13 ___ and tell
19 Mention, with "to"
22 Burrows and Fortas
25 Sailor's sheet
26 Chukkers, in polo
27 ___ of vipers
28 Once called the Gold Coast
30 TV or computer mode
31 Code for letter R
32 Used with crazy and fry
33 British fellow
35 Cricket sound
38 Old prescription for a depressed lady
41 Small arthropods
44 Releases
45 Lady's undergarment
48 Computer display area
50 Take by legal authority
53 Ratio of probability
54 Kind of moss
55 Raines or Fitzgerald
56 Colored
58 Ingredient of human kindness?
59 Harry's wife
61 British nap
62 Make last
64 Used with conservative or classic

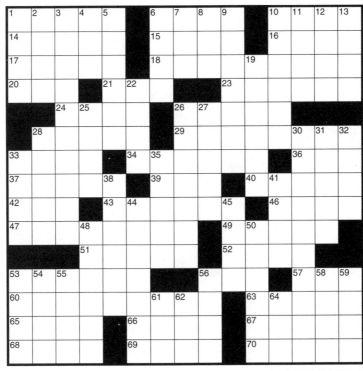

ANSWER, PAGE 60

9

Rhyming Teasers

ACROSS

1 TV's Jack and family
6 Snow vehicle
10 Inquires
14 Like draught beer
15 Bosc or Anjou
16 Knee-bend, in ballet
17 Tiny cat morsel
19 Price scale
20 Greek letter
21 Pale
22 Duplicated
24 Ms. Caldwell and others
26 Human ___
27 Comedians?
30 Sticky stuff
33 Ali ___
36 As ___: generally
37 A king of Judah
38 Worship
40 Mineo
41 More rational
43 Neither's companion
44 Musical bell sound
46 Bus. executives
47 Compass pt.
48 Bachelor pad?
51 "Sturm und ___"
53 Covered with vapor
57 Expand or widen
59 Animal pouch
60 New York city
61 English river
62 American cheese and French toast?
66 Shopper's place
67 Disapproving sounds
68 One-___: partial
69 Terminates
70 Slangy affirmation
71 Lock of hair

DOWN

1 Pig's places?
2 Singer Baker
3 Rose fragrance
4 "I smell a ___"
5 "The ___ Loved Me"
6 Twirl
7 Tennis call
8 Consume
9 Battery part
10 Pre-feminists' symbol
11 Offbeat word group?
12 Flying object
13 Germ
18 Luxuriate
23 Favors
25 Slightly open
26 Conductor/ composer Pierre
28 Alleviating
29 Picture holder
31 One who exploits
32 The red planet
33 Destructive thing
34 Fusses
35 Yawning peer?
39 Brilliance
42 Iowa city
45 Best policy
49 Tentmaker
50 Most pleasing
52 Speaks wildly
54 Exchange
55 Bronte's Jane et al.
56 Actions
57 Woman, to 11-Down
58 ___ the Terrible
59 Waist wrapper
63 "___ pasa?"
64 Actress Hagen
65 Coniferous tree

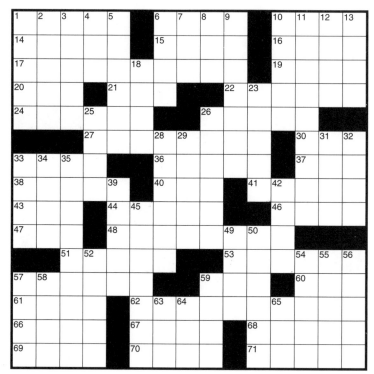

ANSWER, PAGE 62

10

Working Hours

ACROSS

1 A Huntley
5 On the ___: going to the dogs
10 Facile
14 Fabulist
15 Delight in
16 Painter Bonheur
17 Hairdo
18 Literary composition
19 Rain type
20 Unanticipated income
23 "___ De-Lovely": Porter song
24 Caboodle's chum
25 Baby rocker
29 Papal document
31 Belgian commune
34 Push back
35 Come-on
36 ___ to question: unsure
37 Toiler's Utopia?
40 Entertainer Adams
41 Horse d'oeuvre?
42 Flinch
43 ___ Monte, CA
44 Parisian priest
45 Fondled
46 Capp's Abner
47 Hupmobile, e.g.
48 Drudgery after dark?
56 Corn or wheat
57 Hauled
58 Where Bhutan is
59 Diamond delights
60 Figure of speech
61 Prefix with jack or stick
62 Church's altar end
63 Reeled in lampreys
64 Rozelle

DOWN

1 Kind of hammer
2 Sound system
3 Make
4 Walked on
5 Composed
6 Marx and Malden
7 Type of type: Abbr.
8 Unload
9 Firework
10 Extortion
11 Places
12 What time ___?
13 South Dakota's ___ Lands
21 Horse
22 Artist's medium
25 Dogma
26 "The Cloister and the Hearth" author
27 Month
28 Take out
29 Montana city
30 Novelist Leon
31 Exhausted
32 Pennies, in Bristol
33 Coughed up, in poker
35 Goneril's father
36 Neglect
38 Gambling game
39 Jugs
44 XXVI quadrupled
45 Softly lined
46 Decline
47 ___ suzette
48 Valise
49 Molders
50 Time long past
51 Army truant
52 Metal fastener
53 Key
54 Decree
55 Record
56 Half of a dance

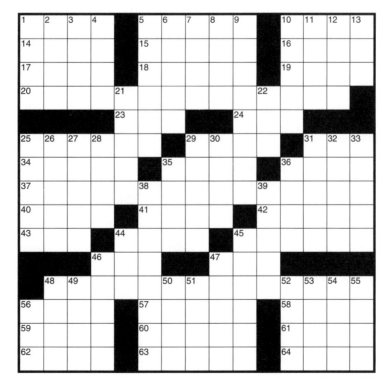

ANSWER, PAGE 64

11

Heads Up

ACROSS

1 Lorre's sleuth role
5 Voice
10 Talks
14 Always
15 King of Tyre
16 Marc's lover
17 Swimming pool
19 Dregs
20 Bullfight cry
21 Space
22 In time: Music
24 Statutes
25 Clip
26 Earthenware
29 Moist medicinal mass
33 Ring bearers
34 Revolt
35 Weir
36 Book of the Bible
37 Inn
38 Ascend
39 Born
40 Spanish composer
41 Cite as evidence
42 Filmy thread
44 One-horse sleigh
45 Greek god of love
46 Golf pegs
47 North American aboriginal
50 Spoken
51 Be in debt
54 Nullify
55 Tito's legacy
58 English queen
59 Muse of memory
60 Saucy
61 Yuletide
62 Oozes
63 Very, in Versailles

DOWN

1 Less: Music
2 Ellipse
3 Head, in Paris
4 Money of Anglo-Saxon England
5 Summer wear
6 Wearies
7 Song
8 Greek letter
9 The Messiah, to some
10 Named: Obs.
11 Turkish flag
12 Retain
13 Indifferent
18 Brads
23 Cultivate the soil
24 Experts
25 Staid
26 Belfry sound
27 A lover
28 Double-reed instruments
29 Apostle
30 Moron
31 Social class
32 Arab prince
34 Parts
37 Namesakes
38 Grooves
40 ___ Delano Roosevelt
41 Put down
43 Large beer mug
44 Discontinues
46 Trample
47 First czar of Russia
48 "That's a ___"
49 Eat
50 Double curve
51 It's past
52 Metal rope
53 Food
56 One, in Paris
57 To the point

ANSWER, PAGE 56

12

Furtive Moves

ACROSS
1 Victor from France
5 Out of sight: French
10 Dangle
14 Corrida shouts
15 Rigel's constellation
16 Scrooge, briefly
17 In search of prey
19 Naldi of the silents
20 Bignoniaceous tree
21 Most proximate
23 Attention-getter
24 Model Carol's namesakes
26 Irving or Madigan
27 Cinematic event
32 Kind of bowl or bar
35 Cravings
36 Workout site
37 Blackhearted
38 Nightwear, briefly
39 Anted up
40 Sleep stage, for short
41 Light bulb, comics style
43 Jouster's weapon
44 Taxpayer's bane
48 Ump kin
49 Honor
50 Wake-up hrs.
53 Offered counsel
57 Assyrian capital
59 Grasslands
60 Storage area
62 Lion's pride
63 Anatomical tissues
64 Story starter
65 Stout relatives
66 Influences
67 Headliner

DOWN
1 Moonshine
2 Radius neighbors
3 Museum founder J. Paul
4 Job-safety grp.
5 Heave in irregular manner
6 Book boo-boos
7 "Blame It on ___"
8 Like this entry
9 Forget, sort of?
10 Agincourt victor
11 Rose's love
12 Garden State cagers
13 Small pest
18 African ruminant
22 City near Des Moines
25 Airplane seizure
27 Gal of song
28 Foot: Latin
29 "No man ___ island"
30 Majestic
31 Baseball's Boggs
32 Belgrade native
33 Declare
34 Peru bean town?
38 Apple of one's eye
39 Mush or mash
41 Tina's ex et al.
42 Lemon features
43 Spinks and Redbone
45 Emergencies
46 Airport feature
47 Roman officials
50 ___-garde
51 Kaaba site
52 Diaphanous
53 Soprano Gluck
54 Distribute cards
55 Weathercock
56 A Barrymore
58 Poetry collection
61 Chicken-king linkage

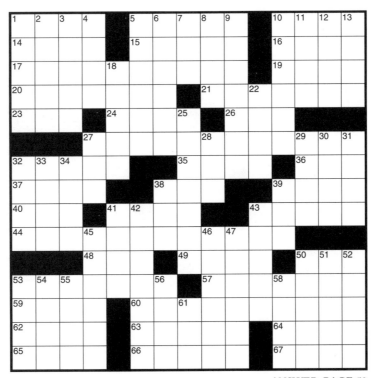

ANSWER, PAGE 58

13

Dexterity

ACROSS

1 Former Secretary of State
5 Explorer De ___
9 "___ a Kick Out of You"
13 Movie dog
14 Porch
15 Moved with haste
16 Is in control
19 Song of praise
20 Winding
21 Links grp.
22 Relative of et al.
23 Words of resignation
32 Heartbeat
33 State bird of Hawaii
34 Mouths
35 Let it stand
36 Took out
37 Kind of corner
38 Salt Lake City athlete
39 Iota
40 Step
41 Fails to applaud
45 Thatcher et al.
46 Arnold of WWII fame
47 Outdoor
51 Novelist Calvino
54 Prompting revelation
57 Jai ___
58 Carries
59 Rara avis
60 ___ Myra Hess
61 Span. ladies
62 All seven

DOWN

1 Exclamation of triumph
2 Relative of PDQ
3 "___ Lovely Day Today"
4 Portal pole
5 Erwin of old movies
6 Expression of chagrin
7 Antelope
8 Watchful
9 Home of Ulysses
10 Hero's counterpart
11 Lightweight champ of yore
12 Actor Danson
14 French upper house
17 The ___, Netherlands
18 Roman
23 301 B.C. battle site
24 All together, in music
25 Winter hazard
26 ___ a customer
27 Criminal
28 Muse of memory
29 Julius, e.g.
30 Fear
31 Tommy of song
36 "Thés ___": afternoon dances
37 Western tribesmen
40 "___ what you think!"
42 Coin
43 Atlanta arena
44 Recoils
47 Oop's mate
48 Carriage in Hyde Park
49 Stravinsky
50 Composer Nino ___
52 Bowling alley
53 Draft classification
54 Craze
55 Nintendo's Super ___
56 AMA members

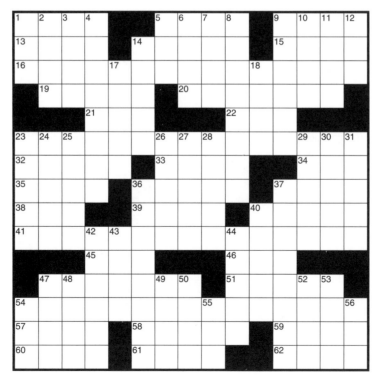

ANSWER, PAGE 60

14

'Round the Clock

ACROSS

1 "Laughing Cavalier" painter
5 Trade punches
9 St. Louis team
13 On the briny
14 Strident noise
15 Theater sign
16 James Baldwin opus
19 Lover's song
20 Flight part
21 Bill Mauldin subjects
22 Where Meaux is
24 Fireplace adjunct
28 Cattle calls
29 Circumference segment
32 Movie starring Treat Williams
33 Barbizon artist
34 World chess champion, 1960–61
35 Hart-Kaufman collaboration
39 Wade's challenger
40 Relocates
41 Inter ___
42 Quarterback's target
43 Numbers
44 Giggle
46 Long times
47 Poet's contraction
48 Wrap
51 Mamet's "___ Buffalo"
56 Words on a postcard
59 Site of Camus' "The Plague"
60 Like the dawn
61 Summers, in Aix
62 Blanch
63 Priam's realm
64 Clutter

DOWN

1 Bowlers
2 Court figure
3 Villain's trademark
4 Burglar's target
5 Arctic vehicles
6 Window segment
7 Exist
8 "Oedipus ___"
9 Fasten anew
10 Central stem
11 Marceau, e.g.
12 Gang ending
14 Cranium contents
17 "Bus Stop" playwright
18 Schubert's "Valse ___"
22 Becker of tennis
23 Shingle site
24 Durable Dinah
25 Fugue's cousin
26 Did a kitchen chore
27 Palindromic preposition
28 Some spies
29 Inclined
30 Flaxlike fiber
31 Weatherman's word
33 Stalagmite settings
36 "Cymbeline" heroine
37 "And Then There Were ___"
38 Make lace
44 Minute
45 Apropos of
46 Fashion silhouette
47 One of the Brontës
48 Boutique
49 Mitchell plantation
50 Executive office shape
51 Curly topping
52 Gossip tidbit
53 Mention
54 Ed or Leon
55 Monster's loch?
57 Procure
58 Rhine feeder

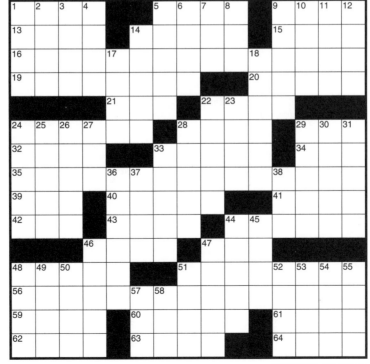

ANSWER, PAGE 62

15

Ranking

ACROSS

1 Soft drinks
6 Contour
11 Era
14 Intermediary
15 Like some seals
16 Filmdom's Chaney
17 Corporal's boss
20 Not kidding
21 Ocean liner
22 Desserts
24 British politician
25 Negligent
29 Certain lizards
33 Writer Turgenev
34 Category
35 Propane
38 Boss of 17-Across
42 Wapiti
43 Bakery items
44 Nick Charles' dog
45 Golfer's feat
46 TV's Dan
48 Lalapalooza
51 Weight unit
53 Ziegfeld revues
57 Mean
62 Boss of 38-Across
64 Compass pt.
65 Follow
66 Twilled cloth
67 Legal thing
68 Facilitated
69 Keyholes, e.g.

DOWN

1 Weakens
2 Make eyes
3 Costly
4 Opponent
5 Small porches
6 Intelligence
7 ___-been: old-timer
8 God of war
9 Saucy
10 Rim
11 Texas shrine
12 Doomed one
13 Item on a list
18 French affirmatives
19 Road sign
23 Hardened
25 Widespread
26 Pernicious
27 A Gospel author
28 Office-holders
30 Responsibility
31 Craft
32 Ruby or Sandra
34 Fish's organ
35 Long, deep cut
36 Feed the kitty
37 ___-of-Bethlehem
39 ___ la la
40 Woodshed item
41 "King" Cole
45 Author Gardner
46 Favorable review
47 Improves
48 Present
49 Racket
50 Leprechauns
52 Stormed
54 Crystal-gazer's words
55 Volcano
56 Lip
58 Stagger
59 Cartoonist Peter
60 Trot or canter
61 Large trees
63 Aromatic plant

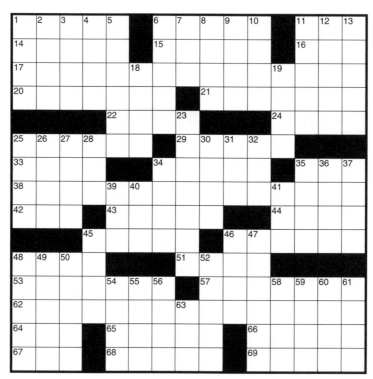

ANSWER, PAGE 56

16
'Tis the Season

ACROSS
1 Wilkes-___, PA
6 The President et al.
10 Pudding ingredient
14 Profit
15 Fairway club
16 Place west of Nod
17 Braga of films
18 Space agcy.
19 Part of Santa's neighborhood
20 "___ before Christmas ..."
23 Great ending
24 Doctrine
25 Weird
29 "___ was stirring ..."
33 Dutch painter
36 Corrode
37 Spoil
38 Weapons
39 Author of quotes
41 Lorre role
42 Actress Zetterling
43 Abbreviated gender
44 Passengers
45 "... hung ___ with care"
49 State of India
50 Loser to DDE
51 Mrs. Charles portrayer
54 "... St. Nicholas soon ___"
59 Sale caveat
62 Orifice
63 Ancient Greek colony
64 Spike
65 Spoken
66 Lodes
67 "Ain't She Sweet" composer
68 New Jersey team
69 Max of painting

DOWN
1 Sew or cook
2 Acknowledges
3 Attacked on the gridiron
4 Social reformer Jacob ___
5 Reaction to Santa's visit?
6 Movie house
7 Barkley of boxing
8 Word in a Mozart title
9 Obstacle
10 Santa's deer minus one
11 Christmas activity?
12 Stage-light gadget
13 No chaser
21 Presidential monogram
22 Pressure of sorts
26 Hearsay
27 Furious
28 Names of Finns like Saarinen
29 Big inits. in video games
30 Irises
31 Capek play
32 Nationality ending
33 Carioca dance
34 Salvers
35 Exudes
39 Singer Davis
40 Kosh preceder in Wisconsin
41 Time of the Bull
43 Note
44 Like Christmas?
46 Rope
47 Mercer et al.
48 Born
51 Vladimir Ilyich Ulyanov
52 Namesakes of a Mannon
53 Leaven
55 Atop
56 Knowledge
57 Mild oath
58 Gardener?
59 Words with mode
60 Droop
61 Diamonds, to Legs

ANSWER, PAGE 58

17

Equine

ACROSS
1 Tenuous fragment
5 Fling
9 Flower
14 Pilaster
15 Potpourri
16 Novelist Jules
17 Boy's name
18 Scrape
19 Musical composition
20 Be patient
23 Fabricate
24 Black Sea port
25 Fortify
27 Mosaic piece
31 Delude
35 Jewish month
36 Leftovers, sometimes
37 Fear
40 Playing cards
41 ___ breve
42 Backdrop
44 Most humble
48 Age
49 Mountain roads
51 Japanese immigrant
55 Pester relentlessly
59 Scoop
60 "Picnic" playwright
61 FDR's pet
62 System
63 Employer
64 Rose oil: Var.
65 Hosiery mishaps
66 Difficulty
67 Frisk

DOWN
1 Do the dishes
2 Under one's guidance
3 Banal
4 Bear of sorts
5 Stymied
6 Wings: Latin
7 Fraidy-cat
8 Formal headgear
9 Wards off
10 Annuls
11 Constant
12 Closes
13 North Dakota Indian tribe
21 Elliptical
22 Jai alai exclamation
26 Blemish
28 Inspector
29 Piquant
30 Flatboat
31 Virile
32 Ait
33 "Move it!"
34 ___ Moines
36 Exhibitionist
38 Tennis score
39 Those who mock
43 Ogden ___
45 Compounds
46 Govt. agency
47 Rat race
50 Import
52 Up to now
53 Muse
54 Muslim faith
55 As big as a ___
56 Icelandic literature
57 Ripens
58 Wyatt
59 ___ Alamos

ANSWER, PAGE 60

18

Hall of Fame Monikers

ACROSS

1 Doorpost
5 Strawberry bunch
9 Baseball stats
13 Track
14 Pacific island
15 Many eras
16 Latvian capital
17 "Tubby the Tuba" writer
18 Immense
19 Joe DiMaggio
22 Sister's daughter
23 Hatfield namesakes
25 Babe Ruth
30 Needlefish
33 It's made by a jerk
34 Accomplishments
35 Atoll
37 Little one
38 Cinder
39 Tomato salad
41 Hollywood heavy
43 Round Table memb.
44 Frankie Frisch
48 ___ a poke
49 The Little Colonel
52 Charlie Gehringer
57 "___ Girl"
59 Maine college town
60 Chess play
61 Place for pins
62 Ladies' knights
63 Nice summers
64 Navy off.
65 Bustle
66 Try

DOWN

1 Actor Victor ___
2 Birdlike
3 Great, in combinations
4 Amanda and Robert
5 Singer from "Dallas"
6 Jannings of old movies
7 Antelope or sun hat
8 Lesbos poetess
9 Football maneuvers
10 Atlantic City promenade
11 Elected ones
12 Fast plane
14 Some stocks and bonds
20 Shield of yore
21 Powder ___
24 Man's adversary
26 Kind of pole
27 Hitler
28 Concerning birth
29 NCO
30 Tennis great
31 Fabulist
32 Censure
36 Nervous one
40 Stylish
42 Imelda or Ferdinand
45 Danish island
46 The Baltic is one
47 Grid wear
50 Cuffed
51 Drop preceder
53 Buck chaser
54 Lille is its capital
55 ___-Iranian
56 Kind of egg
57 RN dispensation
58 Radio man

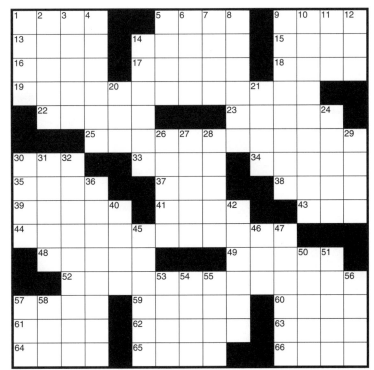

ANSWER, PAGE 62

23

19

Canine

ACROSS

1 Coin receptacle
5 Hayworth and Gam
10 Harmonize
14 Hawaiian city
15 Useful
16 Presley, to some
17 Congregation's response
18 Fragment
19 Actress Patricia
20 Fabulist Aesop's canine
23 Islet
24 Bread spread
25 Boggy
28 Butane, for one
30 Employed
34 Uganda's Amin
35 California's Big ___
36 St. ___: legendary martyr
37 Sultry weather
41 Cancels
42 Actress Farrow
43 Fall mo.
44 Office worker, for short
45 Jazz instrument, briefly
46 Small pies
48 Biting insect
50 Melody
51 Long, drawn-out tale
58 Fly high
59 Arrange in order
60 Notion
61 Novelist Wiesel
62 ___ Haute, IN
63 Suture
64 Had on
65 Senator Kefauver
66 Recipe measures: Abbr.

DOWN

1 Herring's relative
2 Long car, for short
3 Designer Cassini
4 Gin mates
5 Corroded
6 Yen
7 Retread
8 Los ___, NM
9 Flower part
10 Warmongering
11 ___ fixe
12 Pig's relative
13 Building wing
21 Negative vote
22 India's first prime minister
25 All he touched turned to gold
26 Suffix meaning tooth
27 Actress Hasso
28 Songwriter Kahn
29 Fragrance
31 Hearsay
32 Choose
33 Pub game
35 Method: Abbr.
36 "Born in the ___"
38 Blue jean
39 Get ___: be compatible
40 Mend
45 Fashions
46 Poetic contraction
47 Sculptor
49 Child's marble
50 Choreographer de Mille
51 Aria, for one
52 Long-running musical
53 Malicious gossip
54 Fairy tale villain
55 Lyric poetry
56 Harvest
57 Sweet potatoes
58 Baste

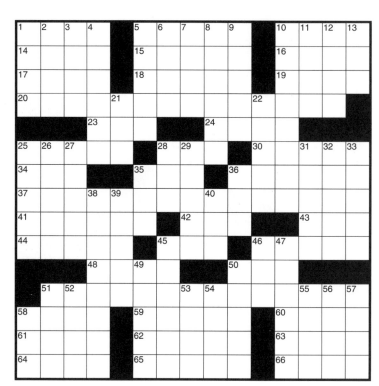

ANSWER, PAGE 56

20

Calendar Change

ACROSS

1 Prevents
5 Newsman Huntley
9 Plane front
13 Out of whack
14 Eater: Suffix
15 Sir Anthony's earldom
16 A Turner
17 "Giuditta" composer
18 Madrid movies
19 What 37-Across is
22 Use a pouf
23 Stand out
24 Grand
29 Splits to splice
33 Flurry
34 Mark up copy
36 Employed
37 See 52-Across
41 They bode
42 Goneril's dad
43 Okhotsk, for one
44 ___ one's laurels
46 Quite audible
49 Yet again
51 Whiz
52 With 12-Down, see 37-Across
59 Fine cherry
60 Housebroken
61 Poi source
62 EPA expert
63 Deviltry
64 Ceaselessly
65 Chromosome unit
66 Dingle
67 Pigeonhole locale

DOWN

1 Vespertilians
2 Deplaned
3 Author Jaffe
4 Few and far between
5 Kitchen king
6 Guffaw
7 Quaint expletives
8 Cylindrical
9 Pasta
10 "Metamorphoses" poet
11 Zilch
12 See 52-Across
14 Cabalist
20 Opposite of 'tain't
21 West of NV
24 Important
25 "There Is Nothing Like ___"
26 Bandsman Spike
27 Bucolic interlude
28 Adduces
30 Cash stash
31 Krupp locale
32 ___ odds
35 One yonder
38 Sort out
39 ___ man: unanimously
40 Gofer business
45 Cleared
47 ___ on parle ...
48 Made a mark on
50 Drive carelessly
52 Appealing
53 Privy
54 Hollywood's Jannings
55 TV's Carter
56 Chalet feature
57 Very, in Ivry
58 1941 Gary Cooper role
59 Seek baksheesh

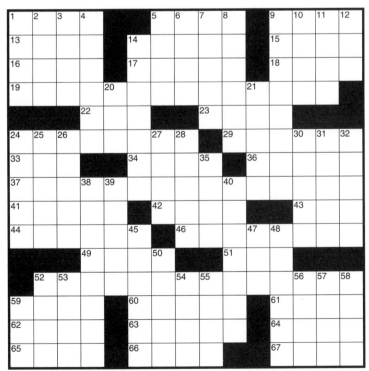

ANSWER, PAGE 58

21

Two/Two

ACROSS
1 Trolley sound
6 Rights org.
10 Campus locale
14 Cowboy flick
15 Early on
16 The Cadets, for short
17 Cowboy's cayuse
18 Belgradian
19 Prolific auth.
20 Art-rocker Brian
21 Exploited
23 Elia's output
25 Pesky insect
26 Laugh
27 Ailment
30 Waterfall
34 Discomfit
35 Established
36 Grassy stretch
37 Computer chip
38 Spaghetti sauce spice
40 Pool length
41 Ms. Hogg
42 "The Balcony" author
43 Ownership query
45 Shortened
47 Let up
48 Come-on
49 Have the facts
50 Quail groups
53 Hoodoo
54 Greek letter
57 NYSE neighbor
58 Convey by car
60 Like some walls
62 Infrequent
63 Vivacity
64 Dame lead-in
65 Volstead supporters
66 NL team
67 Looks upon

DOWN
1 Deal with
2 Reclined
3 ___ time: never
4 Clear profit
5 Timely observance
6 Tact, for one
7 Collegian
8 Singer Denise
9 Without a loss
10 Sky sighting
11 The Middies, for short
12 Xiamen, formerly
13 Rather and Dailey
22 Pipe up
24 Timely activity?
25 Fill the tank, with "up"
26 Gives it a whirl
27 Actress Ouspenskaya
28 Nuclear device
29 Truman's birthplace
30 Shut up
31 Apportion
32 Leave off
33 Not live
35 "Western Star" poet
39 Cash stash
44 Hem's tag-along
46 Alpine animals
47 Ms. Jillian
49 Potters' ovens
50 NL-er
51 Quatrain master
52 Utter
53 Steinbeck hero
54 Storied hotel
55 On earth
56 Pindar's forte
59 Corrida cheer
61 USIA arm

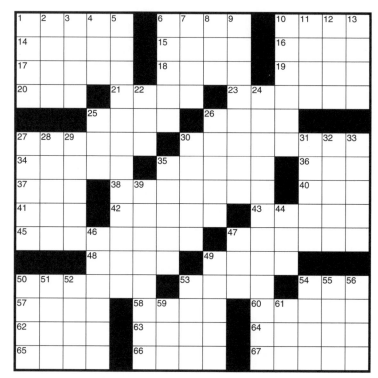

ANSWER, PAGE 60

22

Overage

ACROSS

1 SA rodent
5 Well-fleshed
10 Initials on a card
14 Bristol's river
15 Lumberjacks' competition
16 Spread
17 Not on tape
18 Crushes
20 Manages
22 Street sign
23 Wander
24 Kitchen feature
25 South Americans
27 Hams it up
31 Musical piece
32 Become indistinct
33 Stage fare
34 Elongated fish
35 Seed coverings
36 Exist
37 French islands
39 Italian numeral
40 De Leon
42 Precedent establisher
44 Got hold of
45 ___ of thumb
46 Execrate
47 Make glad
50 Triumph
54 Find again
56 Declare to be so
57 Opposed: Slang
58 ___ Waterways, Canada
59 Waterless
60 Bon ___
61 Classifies
62 Very: French

DOWN

1 ___ Alto
2 Tel ___
3 Shelters
4 ___ barometer
5 Introductions
6 Abiding affection
7 Noun endings
8 Mal de ___
9 Patisserie items
10 "Ivanhoe" heroine et al.
11 Big bunch
12 ___ Cruz
13 Bouquet item
19 Lulu
21 Sensible
24 Small egg
25 Make tracks
26 "... ___ told by an idiot ..."
27 Popular garnish
28 Transfer
29 Flambeau
30 Dessert
32 Scottish dish
35 Selected passages
38 Melodies
40 TV's Jack
41 Friendless
43 "*#@!"
44 Hard rocks
47 Baby-buggy, in Soho
48 ___ mutton
49 Blue-pencil
50 Done
51 Outlet
52 Additional
53 Farm animals
55 ___ y plata

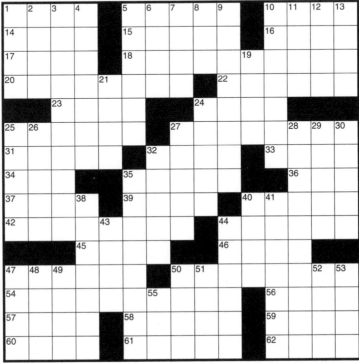

ANSWER, PAGE 62

23

Wall Street

ACROSS

1 ___ assets: accounting entry
6 Concerning
10 Musical finish
14 ___ Arledge of ABC News
15 Dealership, in securities
16 Chief of the Aesir
17 Sailboat
18 Window part
19 Straight
20 Shares sold, less than round
23 "Where the Boys ___"
24 Certain hog
25 Cul. measure
28 Bath powder
31 Some of 51-Across
35 Longfellow town
37 Broker's cold-call hope
39 About: Latin
40 What a margin player doesn't want
43 UT city
44 Forked-tailed hawk
45 Aunts, in Mexico
46 Business pressure, sometimes
48 Soybean product sold on the CBT
50 Abbr. for certain balloons
51 Some are cpls.
53 Bro's sib
55 Top of the list of high-volume securities
63 Margarine
64 Sugar source
65 Buddhist gateway
66 Mythomaniac
67 ___ College, NC
68 Clean the slate
69 Small boat
70 Income for some, expense for others
71 CSA signature

DOWN

1 Approximately
2 Spread a rumor
3 Stove canopy
4 ___ Gay, historic B-29
5 Company publication for stockholders
6 Vipers
7 Former Persian ruler
8 Up ___: so far
9 "Norma" and "Aida"
10 Squeeze
11 Musical halls of old
12 One way to call a broker
13 Pay to play
21 Goad
22 Use transparent paper
25 Packs, as a pipe
26 Begin
27 Before
29 Tall and lean
30 Insurance ___
32 Object of a quest
33 Fanfare
34 Mambo-like dance
36 Stock in a warehouse
38 Grafted, in heraldry
41 Scarpia's killer
42 Stop
47 Pelé's sport
49 Pioneer of antiseptic surgery
52 Trite
54 Something to mind
55 Penicillin producer
56 Mishmash
57 Scorch
58 Privy to
59 Suit jacket feature
60 Certain surgeon
61 Example
62 Patella location

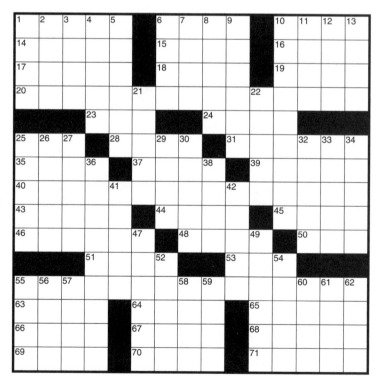

ANSWER, PAGE 56

24

Slapstickers

ACROSS

1 Convex or zoom
5 Desire
9 Baseman's bane
14 "Dies ___"
15 Kuwait VIP
16 Get the suds out
17 It could be floppy
18 Places
19 Wax eloquent
20 The Tramp
23 Gist of a matter
24 Believer: Suffix
25 Some
26 Great clown of the silents
32 Japanese statesman
33 Precious
34 Grating
38 Baby talk
40 Truck stop
43 Party-pooper
44 Pottery fragment
46 Quick try
48 Broadcast
49 Slapstick troupe
53 Fitting
56 Fast flier
57 AL, FL, GA, VA et al.
58 Stars of "Block-Heads"
64 Relatively far-removed
65 Trim
66 "West Side Story" Jet
68 Parade feature
69 One not to be believed
70 Story
71 Painters' aids, for short
72 Pollster Roper
73 Watched carefully

DOWN

1 Cover
2 Sevareid
3 "The Rainmaker" playwright
4 Line meeting a curve
5 Raised properly
6 Mine, to Marcel
7 Pleasant
8 A Nixon
9 Maker
10 Drooping
11 ___ Gay
12 Miss Duke's ex
13 Very small
21 Regretted
22 FDR's successor
26 Auction nods
27 Bryce Canyon is here
28 Fountain treat
29 Trombonist Winding
30 Surrealist painter Max
31 Capture
35 Fair
36 Support
37 Hedge shrubs
39 Refuge
41 DDE's area of command
42 Mexican animal farmer
45 One might get them, just
47 He kisses, in Spanish
50 Designer's initials
51 Fastener
52 A martial art
53 Into the air
54 Actress Prentiss
55 Special teacher
59 Harvest
60 Many a picture-hanger
61 Small amount
62 Low, sturdy cart
63 Streep's alma mater
67 "And so to ___ ..."

ANSWER, PAGE 58

25

By George

ACROSS
1 Exhilarated
5 Upright
9 Ancient Britons
14 Punjab moneybags
15 Las Vegas posting
16 ___ in the dark
17 Single
18 Ma Bell's boy
19 Classical pillar
20 Nature's ingredients for scotch
23 Part of RV
24 Estuary
25 Genetic initials
26 Chichi
27 Reporter
31 To no avail
33 Baseball stat
34 Aviator Balbo
37 Corroded
40 Some radios, for short
41 One from Reno
43 Charles or Milland
44 US resort lake
46 Put up
47 "... ___ I saw Elba"
48 Part of MIT
50 Freshman, e.g.
52 Sugar source
54 Surprised cries
57 Cash stash, briefly
58 Quiche need
59 George's home
64 ___ voce
66 Bog
67 Manned a loom
68 Bellowing
69 Rock star, to some
70 Words of ken
71 Cordillera
72 Withhold
73 Wimp's kin

DOWN
1 Chuck-wagon fare
2 Cantrell or Turner
3 Open some
4 Prime-time soap
5 Friend for fun
6 Unctuous
7 Nasty expression
8 Singer Michelle Shocked, for one
9 "Lang syne"
10 Believer
11 George's planting
12 Realty notice
13 Actor Keach
21 Prized furs
22 Capuchin monkey
26 ___ brochette
27 Tidy
28 Writer Bombeck
29 George's name
30 Church feature
32 Bridgework
35 Gibbon
36 Pindar's forte
38 Turn a penny
39 Security Council vote
42 In high gear
45 Person
49 Excessively
51 Noted evolutionist
52 Romero or Chavez
53 Mall of yore
55 Like monsoon time
56 Malicious
59 To boot
60 Disney sci-fi flick
61 Pry
62 Through
63 Desideratum
65 Label

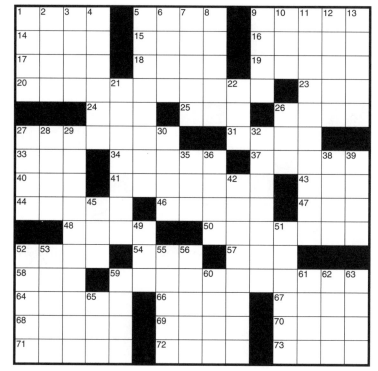

ANSWER, PAGE 60

26

Piquant Places

ACROSS

1 Dispenser of T.L.C., in the Orient
5 UK TV network
8 Beginning
13 San ___, Italian resort
14 Authentic
16 Wed
17 Kind of 42-Across
19 Places for chapeaux
20 Made amends
21 Marlene's costar in "The Blue Angel"
23 Superlative ending
24 Corrida cheer
25 ___ Open: PGA event
27 Suspect's need
30 Kind of 42-Across
34 "The ___ Star": 1957 film
35 Entered
39 River to the English Channel
40 Within: Prefix
42 Zesty food ingredient
43 Wrinkle
44 "Happy Days ..." writer
45 Apprehend
47 "___ It Be": Beatles song
48 Boston neighborhood
50 "... ___ a different drummer ...": Thoreau
52 What it's good to be up to
54 Actor Danson
55 ABA member
58 Cupid
59 Capital of 70-Across
63 West Indian aborigine
65 Kind of 42-Across
67 1955 Glenn Ford movie
68 Kind of tape, for short
69 Hall-of-Famer Graham
70 French department
71 Compass dir.
72 Bootleggers' nemesis

DOWN

1 Chest
2 Companion of potatoes
3 Firepower, for short
4 Socialize
5 Bouquet tosser
6 Rock preceder
7 Like zoo denizens
8 Renegade
9 Compass dir.
10 Position
11 Vous ___
12 Try
15 Frozen dessert
18 Memento
22 Rich and Papas
26 Angle iron
27 On ___: raising Cain
28 Speech
29 Type of card
31 Soft-palate part
32 Grimsby or Mudd
33 Biting insects
36 Medicinal plant
37 Les Paul's partner
38 Fr., Eng. et al.
41 Globes
46 Topic
49 Incapable
51 Famed inventor
53 Cleaving tools
54 Lake ___, NV
55 Bible book
56 Edible root
57 Neat
60 Major chaser
61 NJ five
62 Happy signs for angels
64 "___ the very model ..."
66 Metric measures: Abbr.

ANSWER, PAGE 62

27

Taking a Chance

ACROSS

1 Shot, for short
5 Tin Pan Alley grp.
10 Mole
13 Take an oath
14 Bête chaser
15 Trouble
16 Stocks of dubious worth
18 Ages upon ages
19 Pro nobis lead-in
20 One-third of a 1970 movie title
21 Says
23 Opens the door to
25 Substance
26 Length times width

27 Business actions
30 Kind of millionaire
33 Bowling item
34 Tuck's pal
35 "___ was saying ..."
36 Small amounts of stock
40 Ms. Tanguay
41 Nec.
42 Charles or Bolger
43 Heron's kin
45 Enjoyed the ocean
48 Mont Buet is one
50 Author Murdoch

51 Detergent
55 Extends
57 Ananias
58 Past
59 Here, in Le Havre
60 Best price quotation
63 "___ As a Stranger"
64 Eagle's perch
65 "Some of ___ Days"
66 "Have you ___ wool?"
67 "___ Along the Mohawk"
68 Bridge position

DOWN

1 In the know

2 Kind of music
3 Bell and Kettle
4 "Israel in Egypt," for one
5 Genoese admiral Doria
6 Fountain treats
7 Labor org.
8 Refutation
9 Tease
10 Added inducement
11 Bond rating
12 Itches
13 Harbor sight
17 "Caro ___," Verdi aria
22 Label

24 Garfield, for one
27 "O Sole ___"
28 Split
29 Quarrel
30 Chagall
31 Unscrupulous person
32 Feature of stocks
33 Work at
37 More chic
38 June honoree
39 Distinct
44 Ike, for one
46 Anger
47 Sailor of fiction
48 Straightens
49 Conduct
51 Miner's concern
52 Tokyo quaffs
53 Discharge
54 Motored
55 ___ few, lose a few
56 Sacred image
61 Joanne of Hollywood
62 ___ Na Na

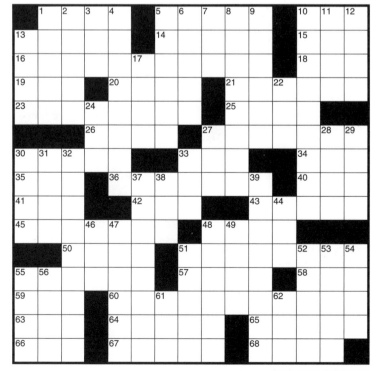

ANSWER, PAGE 57

28

Twosomes

ACROSS
1 Stare in wonder
5 Below cpl.
8 Ash, e.g.
12 Goddess of discord
13 Housetop
15 Chief
16 "... ___ of robins ..."
17 New Rochelle school
18 Spanish river
19 Puppets
22 Waiting room denizens
23 At all, to Keats
26 ___ Lanka
27 Layers
28 Ending for Manhattan
31 Noon, in Nice
34 Golfer with an army
36 Famous adversaries
40 Coeur d'___
41 Ward off
42 Rds.
43 Sam and Miltie
45 Actor Wallach
48 Set of steps
49 Singers like Bing
54 Happily married seniors
56 Actress Daly
59 Persia, today
60 Windy
61 Uris or Spinks
62 Before zwei
63 Buffalo county
64 Suffragist Carrie
65 A Stooge
66 Sever

DOWN
1 Knees: Anat.
2 Common contraction
3 Fish, to Ovid
4 Williams of swim films
5 Copy in block letters
6 Nutriments
7 And or but: Abbr.
8 From ___: since time began
9 Insurgent, for short
10 Musical talent
11 Tokyo, once
14 Gounod opera
16 About: Abbr.
20 Soul
21 ___ Open: PGA event
24 Heaters
25 Leading man of musicals
27 Omen
28 Actress Lupino
29 Anklebone
30 Happening
32 Vb. forms
33 Winner over AES
35 Exclamations of inquiry
37 "Border ___": 1949 movie
38 Street or Reese
39 "___ a Grecian Urn"
44 Weird
46 Boarder
47 Harm
49 Dark blue: Prefix
50 Rajah's mate
51 Silk dye
52 Appraised
53 Curved planking
55 Edge
56 Dispensation from RNs
57 Indeed
58 "Like it or ___!"

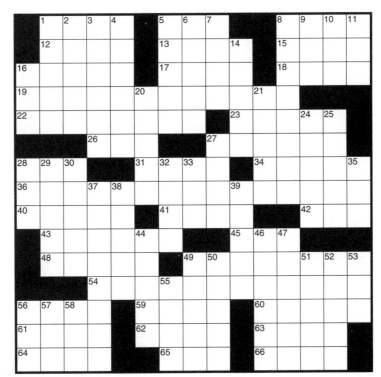

ANSWER, PAGE 59

29

Vintage Theme

ACROSS

1 World holder of renown
6 Colleen
10 ___ E. Lee
14 Nantes' river
15 Field
16 1958 Pulitzer winner in fiction
17 Jordan's capital
18 Family group
19 Erase
20 Early auto racer
23 Bern's river
24 Mérida living room
25 Lean to one side
28 Motion from a yes man
31 Like the fashions fresh from Paris
35 A feast ___ famine
36 Fall potable

38 Flick
39 Armchair strategists, probably
42 Silly
43 Filled up
44 "___ ole davil, sea": O'Neill
45 Stimulus-response device
47 Make a seam
48 City east of Phoenix
49 ___ fours
51 Age for study
53 Coleridge character
60 Othello, for one
61 Meridian

62 Fretted and ___
64 Story start, at times
65 AZ's ex-governor Mecham
66 Vampire
67 Cross
68 Alain-___ Lesage
69 Large antelope

DOWN

1 Mode introducer
2 Egyptian pyramid, e.g.
3 OH city
4 Noah's landing

5 Tropical herb
6 Like certain curtains
7 Woody's boy
8 Pinnipeds
9 Summer footwear
10 Heating unit
11 S-shaped molding
12 Telephone inventor
13 ___ off: drove
21 Pyle or Kovaks
22 Blazed
25 Slow-moving lemur
26 Good-night girl
27 Old Scratch

29 Track probabilities
30 Painter of ballerinas
32 Side-step
33 Eliot's Marner
34 Seed coat
36 Haitian, sometimes
37 Plexus
40 What Erato did for Dante
41 Not as old
46 Part of a sled
48 Teacher's guide
50 Range
52 Ransack
53 Cupid
54 Admonishment from Mom
55 Chanel's nickname
56 Sound of pain
57 English princess
58 Austen novel
59 Check
63 Mom's partner

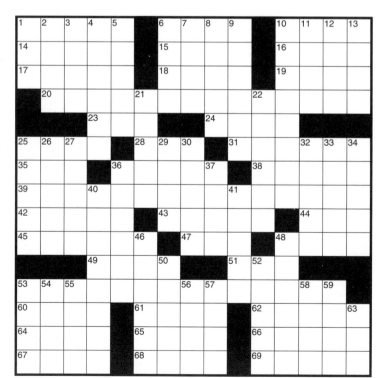

ANSWER, PAGE 61

30

Love

ACROSS

1 "___ Day's Night"
6 Deserved
11 Exclamations of surprise
14 Identified
15 Kind of orange
16 No vote
17 "Thou shalt love ___ as thyself": Romans
19 "___ Wiener Walzer"
20 Comfort
21 Pegs for Peete
22 Saw
24 Pace
26 Part of
27 Thais, e.g.
30 Interpret
34 Lavin of "Alice"
35 Sawyer of TV news fame
36 British institution
37 Wave, to Debussy
38 Big floes
39 "___ Is All I Ask": G. Jenkins
40 Vital statistic
41 Starr of 1-Across
42 Treaty city
43 Grow less
45 Steeples
46 Many eras
47 Fashion name
48 Anouk of the movies
50 Kind of party
52 Actress Garr
56 Director Reiner
57 "Love looks not ___": Shakespeare
60 Broke fast
61 Hip
62 "Rigoletto" composer
63 Tavern
64 ___-eater
65 "... ___ of robins ..."

DOWN

1 Pot builder
2 Sounds of laughter
3 Golfer Alcott and others
4 Fugitive
5 Winner over AES
6 Thesaurus name
7 1975 Wimbledon champ
8 Keep ___ on
9 Self
10 Madden
11 "That ye love ___": John
12 Former Secretary of State
13 New Year's word
18 "How sweet ___!"
23 Knotts or Ho
25 Alicia of "Falcon Crest"
26 Fleming et al.
27 "... like ___ of immortality": Keats
28 Scorch
29 "Will you love me ___ ...?": Walker
30 Lament
31 Famed villain
32 Net
33 Words with Far and Near
35 Lairs
38 Prejudice
39 Baker's dozen
41 Urban ___
42 Main mailing place: Abbr.
44 Fish fledglings
45 Soft sound
47 Appointments
48 Part of UAR
49 Atom
50 RBI, e.g.
51 Way starter
53 Jane of fiction
54 Warren Beatty film
55 "What ___?"
58 ___ Jima
59 A Gabor

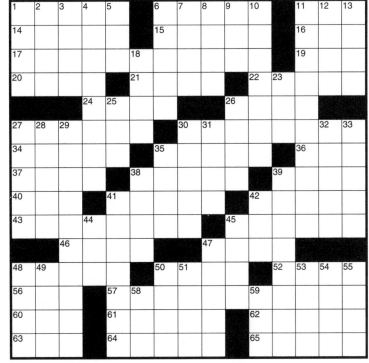

ANSWER, PAGE 63

31

Western Sites

ACROSS

1 Fuddy-duddy
5 Gaucho gear
10 Be loose-tongued
14 Swear
15 Pavarotti's love
16 Highway sector
17 NM tourist attraction
20 Ron or Rick
21 Employ
22 Vicuna's milieu
23 After Mon.
24 Blueblood
26 Deli rolls
29 Actor Peter
32 Wave-tossed
33 Hue
34 Ypres yes
36 Famed wagon route
40 Males
41 Hangs around
42 Pot increment
43 Four-in-hand
45 Execrates
47 Lock location
48 Unaccompanied
49 Peculate
52 Tarry
53 ___ de deux
56 AZ sight
60 Very much
61 It hangs thereby
62 Tatar locale
63 Lacrosse teams
64 Was intrepid
65 Show biz award

DOWN

1 Food fish
2 Stadium shape
3 Small boat
4 Hooter
5 Coddles
6 Bradley and Sharif
7 Mine find
8 Semicircle
9 Lots of water
10 Ore
11 Suet's kin
12 Mrs. Lindbergh
13 Mrs. Truman
18 Rabbi's locale
19 Poltroon
23 Pekoes
24 Turns pages
25 Ye ___ Tea Shoppe
26 Spa structure
27 Pallid
28 Simpletons
29 Tremble
30 Certain horses
31 Ensemble
33 Undress
35 ___ du Vent
37 An antacid
38 Macadamias
39 Uncommon
44 Visual aids
45 Did the hair
46 Biblical preposition
48 Serve soup
49 Argument
50 Part of TV
51 Cap or collar
52 Clothing
53 "Dinero" unit
54 H ___ hotel
55 Hold up
57 Short-lived thing
58 Call ___ day
59 Turncoat

ANSWER, PAGE 57

36

32

Themeless

ACROSS

1 Reproach
6 Less
11 Fracas
14 Rustic
15 Original settler
17 Equipped
18 Pickled
19 Samovar serving
20 Irish hill
21 Drum or fiddle
22 Pastimes
25 Pigeon call
27 Twisted
29 Steel wool, e.g.
33 Future officer
34 Push aside
35 Ex-fighter or soldier
37 Appends
38 Honkers
39 Talk wildly
40 New: Prefix
41 Farm animals
42 Two-headed god
43 Nosy one
45 River of India
46 Western Indian
47 Suit fabric
48 Actress Diana
51 Stack
53 Tennis stroke
56 Inclined to copy
59 Excuse
61 ME lake
62 Western animal
63 Tosspot
64 Plants
65 ___ Park, CO

DOWN

1 The neighbors' kid
2 Inveigle
3 Final conflict
4 West or Clark
5 Ancient times: Poetic
6 Half of a singing group
7 Building beam
8 Fictional Charles
9 Swiss canton
10 Hebrew letter
11 Miss Hayworth
12 Singletons
13 Takes a spouse
16 Hungarian beauty
20 Senator Kennedy
23 Impresses deeply
24 Encountered
25 Volcano shape
26 Not at home
27 Scrutinize
28 Takes on cargo
29 Very thin
30 Swear
31 Billy Graham, e.g.
32 Stage presentation
34 Parched
36 "___ of the D'Urbervilles"
38 Yawn
39 Pealed
41 Witticism
42 Jolt
44 Expels
45 Word with whiz
47 Husky loads
48 Grows faint
49 Melville novel
50 Civil disorder
51 Harbor fixture
52 Russian ruler
54 Hautboy
55 Containers
57 Pershing's men: Abbr.
58 "___ Robe"
59 Honest ___
60 Fleur-de-___

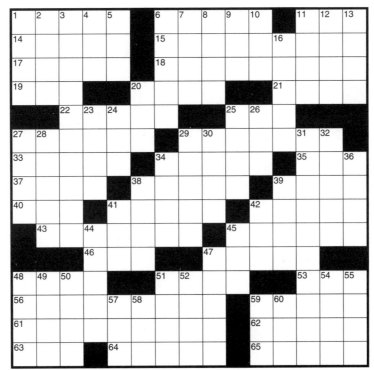

ANSWER, PAGE 59

33

Film Hits

ACROSS

1 Yemenites
6 "Do ___ others ..."
10 Sunken fence
14 Sudden terror
15 Cupola site
16 Mime
17 Oscar-winning film, 1965
20 Bound by an oath
21 NFL team
22 Well-known loch
24 Málaga Mrs.
25 Does weeding
28 Clockmaker Terry
30 Tangles
35 ___-Margret
36 Menial workers
38 Archetype
39 1983 hit film
42 Analyze a sentence
43 Family members: French
44 Jet follower
45 Jacket part
47 Creek
48 Sawbucks
49 "Three Men ___ Tub"
51 Winged
53 Calligraphers' needs
58 Runs
61 Oscar-winning film, 1939
64 OK city
65 Fortuneteller
66 Dangerous mosquito
67 Kids
68 Salver
69 Precipitation

DOWN

1 Befitting
2 Stadium sounds
3 Again
4 Western hoofed animals
5 Twenty
6 Samovar
7 Signals approval
8 Restaurateur Shor
9 Presents
10 Tow
11 Cathedral section
12 Legatee
13 Rainbows
18 Invisible
19 Selfish people
23 Sailing boat
25 Stringed instruments
26 Tatum of films
27 ___ nous
29 Deduce
31 US staff off.
32 Singer Della
33 Burdened
34 Long, narrow cuts
36 Advance showing
37 Thin groove
40 Purpose
41 Well-being
46 Start an army career
48 Mason's tool
50 Modify
52 Zones
53 "___ a Kick Out of You"
54 Something taboo
55 Do needlework
56 Joins together
57 Gooden's turf
59 Flood or ebb
60 Snick-or-___
62 ___ out: test
63 Summer time: Abbr.

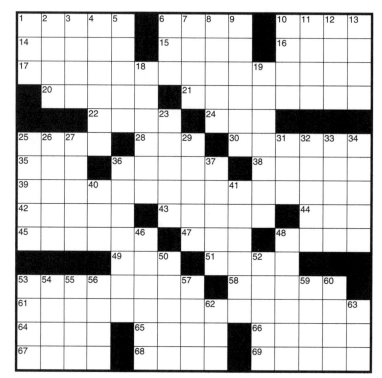

ANSWER, PAGE 61

34

Money Line

ACROSS

1 Links standard
4 Not up yet
8 Muscat's locale
12 Kazan
14 The street, in Strasbourg
16 Central Russian city
17 Dow Jones barometer
19 Followers
20 Made lace
21 Notwithstanding that
23 Russian river
25 "The March King"
26 Esteemed
30 Staggered
33 Friendship
34 Reckless
36 Calendar abbr.
37 Word on a wall
38 Biblical weeds
39 House comm. created in 1938
40 Golfer Hogan
41 Committed a gaffe
42 Parsonage
43 Journalist Fallaci
45 Jogged the memory
47 Tie the knot secretly
49 Circlet
50 Some needlework items
53 Loch monster, familiarly
57 Jai ___
58 Describing some discounted securities
60 Arabian port
61 Pierre's school
62 Buddhist scriptural language
63 Billy or Pete
64 Autocrat
65 Wee bit

DOWN

1 Nuisance
2 Neighbor of Sask.
3 Public disorder
4 Surveyor's instrument
5 Forbid
6 Wagnerian earth goddess
7 Combats for twos
8 Idle
9 Type of shared investment entity
10 Not have ___ to stand on
11 Humorous US poet
13 Cause to happen
15 Obtains by threat
18 MA senator John
22 LA politician Long
24 "The Merry Widow" composer
26 Stallone role
27 UAE potentate
28 Gov't. home mortgage certificates
29 He who challenges
31 Obliterate
32 Cut up into small pieces
35 Passover ceremony
38 Acrobat's apparatus
39 Concludes a call
41 Organic compound
42 Actor Sal
44 Kind of skiing
46 Kitchen gadget
48 Build
50 Former W. German territory
51 Ray or Moro
52 B'way success signs
54 Tiff
55 KS town
56 Locale of Vance Air Force Base
59 Palm leaf

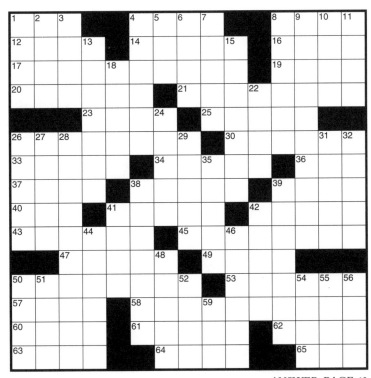

ANSWER, PAGE 63

35

Just So

ACROSS
1 Neth. neighbor
5 Arab garments
9 Hackneyed
14 Soprano Mills
15 Marathon
16 Consumed
17 Balanchine ballet
18 Indian of Machu Picchu
19 Dolts
20 Subject of 38-Across
23 Workers' assn.
24 Symbols on the staff
27 Ultra-smooth
31 Bagnold of "The Chalk Garden"
33 NT book
35 Actor's comment
36 Pet's pest
37 Woody's child
38 Most of a best-selling title
41 Emerald Isle
42 Galatea's lover
43 Lehmann or Lenya
44 Dry, as wine
45 Similar
46 Haunt
47 "The Cloister and the Hearth" author
49 Skater Midori
50 Co-author of 38-Across
57 Famous fabulist
60 Tom Joad, e.g.
61 Cyrano's feature
62 Etching or lithograph
63 Barak of "Die Frau ohne Schatten"
64 Bradley or Sharif
65 ___ Park, CO resort
66 Word on a towel
67 Infamous fiddler

DOWN
1 Necklace part
2 Therefore
3 Bert Lahr role
4 Actress Rowlands
5 Tediously
6 Guitar's cousin
7 Business abbr.
8 Recipe direction
9 Banded together
10 Scrapes
11 Possessive pronoun
12 Kind of shirt
13 USNA grad
21 Rotterdam or QE2
22 Dickens' Heep
25 Cylindrical, but tapered
26 Slapping sounds
27 Gluts
28 More wan
29 Fencing position
30 Zoological suffix
31 Small and spritely
32 Pro basketball team
34 Course features
36 Central points
37 Dos-___: square-dance call
39 Captured
40 Joint
45 Votes to accept
46 Not these
48 Make reparation
49 More like winter
51 Tenth Hebrew letter
52 Tiny terrier
53 Presently
54 "Fanny" composer
55 Moussorgsky's Boris
56 Lowest grade
57 Mimic
58 Hesitant syllables
59 Pose

ANSWER, PAGE 57

36

By George, Part II

ACROSS

1 Bills
5 Cathedral: Italian
10 Scheme
14 Juno
15 Anchor position
16 Hamlet or Macbeth
17 Russia's ___ Mountains
18 Nightingale, for one
19 Burden
20 One of 60 in an hr.
21 He wrote of the cherry tree
23 Nomad
25 Indistinct
26 Over there: Archaic
27 Jester's headgear
32 Gapes
34 Piece of turf
35 Yoko
36 Early Olympic site
37 Swiss mathematician
38 Prince predecessor
39 Chaney
40 Emulate a villain
41 Kind of sack
42 Most wary
44 Gusted
45 Mali's cont.
46 The Old Sod
49 Washington's home
54 "I cannot tell a ___"
55 Hooters
56 Bell town
57 G, F, or C
58 Funnyman Jay
59 Carved post
60 Pilaf ingredient
61 Dutch treat
62 Polishing agent
63 PC operator

DOWN

1 Hitchhike
2 Hawk's home
3 Site of a Washington defeat
4 Gal of song
5 One of an Argos king's 50 daughters
6 Driving maneuver
7 Hockey legend and family
8 Hatred: Prefix
9 Unrestricted access
10 Introductions
11 Solitary
12 Astringent
13 Costner role
21 Equivoques
22 Chamberlain
24 Klutz's outcry
27 ___ mignon
28 Finished
29 General who surrendered to Washington at Yorktown
30 Shortly
31 Menhaden
32 Shout
33 Cosmetic ingredient
34 Charges
37 Devitalize
38 Petrol
40 Separate
41 Valley
43 Kidnapper's demand
44 Abounding in shrubs
46 "___ Sanctum"
47 Relative
48 Put off
49 Type of spy
50 Was indebted
51 Forearm bone
52 Esau
53 Proportion
57 Group of vineyards: French

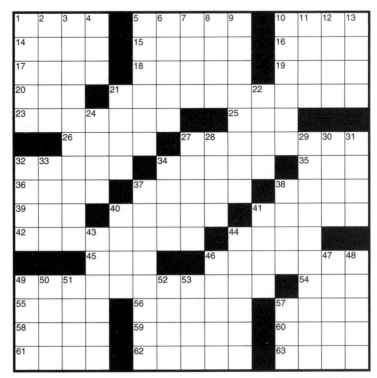

ANSWER, PAGE 59

37

Elevated

ACROSS
1 Tineid, e.g.
5 Wrong
10 Eminence
14 Jai ___
15 Shore of song
16 Conceptuali-
zation
17 Excited
18 Stranded
20 No. 5 iron
22 Radames' love
23 Canal system
24 Card game
26 Updike's
"___: A
Book"
28 Slender
thread
32 Insipid people
35 Chemical
compound

36 ___-do-well
38 Wading bird
40 Birthright
seller
41 Records
43 Chops
44 Baltic natives
46 Ceramic
rectangle
47 Look for
48 Use the gray
matter
50 Carol's best
friend
52 Zola
protagonist
54 Elegance
55 Meyers or
Onassis
58 San ___
60 Baltimore
athlete

64 Scot
67 Minced oath
68 Cosmetic
ingredient
69 Scarsdale and
NutriSystem,
e.g.
70 Before cast or
phone
71 Semester
72 Ranee's garb
73 Bear young

DOWN
1 Word to a
lady
2 Gymnast
Korbut
3 NM resort
4 Pretentious,
to Jethro
5 Supporter

6 1002, to
Brutus
7 ___ Swenson
8 Master, in
Madras
9 Darkened
10 Disencumber
11 Appends
12 Stout's Wolfe
13 Knock out
19 Mother-of-
pearl
21 "___ a
Camera"
25 ___ a time
27 1956 Crosby
film
28 Experience
29 Map's map
30 Reluctant
31 Not so hot
33 Dress up

34 Mended
37 Keepsake
39 Expresses
disapproval
42 Walrus
45 Harsh
utterance
49 Massages
51 Russian farm
village
53 Membranes:
Zool.
55 At the drop
of ___
56 Annoy
57 Borodin's
Prince
59 ___-Neisse
Line
61 S-shaped
curve
62 Tra trailer
63 Paradise
65 Border
66 Summer, for
Saint-Saëns

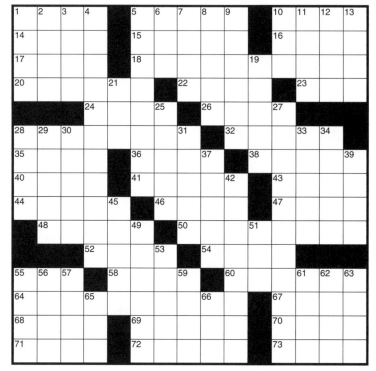

ANSWER, PAGE 61

38

Tourist Stops

ACROSS

1 The Crimson Tide
5 Like some bears
10 Lingerie items
14 Open a bit
15 Miss Rainer
16 Papal curia
17 Golden Gate locale
20 Outer: Prefix
21 Erstwhile
22 Olympian Jesse
23 Canapé topping
24 Opposite of "vive"
26 Goes for a drive
29 Castle features
32 Indigo source
33 Scintillas
34 Charlotte ___
36 Old Faithful locale
40 To boot
41 Raises the hackles
42 Nose out
43 Ten-year periods
45 Tiresome reading
47 Work vehicles
48 Chatter
49 Thwacked
52 TV's Johnson
53 Pro's charge
56 Donald Duck locale
60 Pointless
61 Spud
62 Set the pace
63 Impedimenta
64 Favorite cheese
65 Gainsay

DOWN

1 Establish
2 Trojan War hero
3 ___-war
4 Sandy's word
5 Enroots
6 Pound fraction
7 Parasites
8 "___ was saying ..."
9 Homeowner: Abbr.
10 Shop for a book
11 Stole, e.g.
12 ___ impasse
13 Announces
18 Veldt sound
19 Vulgar
23 Voter's stop
24 Hatchbacks
25 Roughage source
26 Yucatán Indian
27 Upright
28 Diacritical mark
29 Carries
30 Make deals
31 Snorkel or Bilko
33 British ___
35 ___ out: got by
37 Harangued
38 Latitudinous
39 ___ up: liven
44 Sled or boat
45 Bacchus followers
46 Ball of yarn
48 Bo and ti
49 Chug-a-lug
50 Fashioned
51 Paella pot
52 Opponent
53 At large
54 Panache
55 Air swirl
57 Pronoun
58 Bromide
59 Timeworn

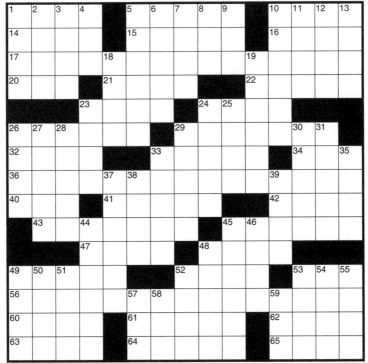

ANSWER, PAGE 63

39

Stately Blooms

ACROSS

1 Swindle
6 Slight breeze
10 Chest coverings
14 January, in Madrid
15 Entertainer Fitzgerald
16 Mine entrance
17 Come to ___
18 Grad
19 Levitate
20 GA state flower
23 ___ Francisco
26 Keep ___ on
27 Scoring-table equipment
28 Expeditions
30 Ice or memorabilia holders
31 ERA, RBI, or BA
32 Philippine city
36 FL state flower

41 West ___
42 Superficial extent
44 Semester marks
48 "My Sister ___"
50 Religious remembrance
51 Helps with a robbery
54 Domain of 64-Across
55 MI state flower
58 Act like a snake
59 Got down from
60 IN state flower
64 Ocean flyer

65 Sagacious
66 American dogwood
67 Suffix with old or young
68 Piercing glance
69 Meadowlands

DOWN

1 ___ culpa
2 Young ___
3 Tennis term
4 FL lake dweller, for short
5 Silken chapeau
6 "Lafayette, ___ here"
7 Mix or debase

8 Stroke of luck
9 Subdued
10 Scottish novelist
11 Dialects
12 Actress Jacqueline
13 TX range animals
21 Naval men
22 Distinguishing character
23 Blks.
24 Detroit product
25 Close at hand
29 NYC's Grand Central ___
30 Recesses for wearing apparel

33 Headed
34 Sash for a geisha
35 ___ de France
37 Family gal
38 "My Gal ___"
39 Mining products
40 Submissive
43 None in particular
44 Embellishes
45 Detailed statement
46 Resembling lofty mountains
47 Comedienne Phyllis
49 Leggy crustacean
51 Yankee fireman Reynolds
52 ID city
53 Fragrant compound
56 Shout
57 AZ city
61 Tulsa product
62 Obituary word
63 Ann. times

ANSWER, PAGE 57

44

40

USA Stars

ACROSS

1 ___ of the law
4 Ed or Nancy
8 Old-hat
13 Opine
15 Upset
16 Musteline mammal
17 Catchall
18 Part of MA's motto
19 Behaves like a frightened horse
20 TV personality
23 "___ we down-hearted?"
24 ___ Jeanne d'Arc
25 Hurry
29 Kind of throat
31 Entrances
34 A charged particle
35 Covering
37 African antelope
38 Certain rags
39 Famed comedienne
42 Daredevil Knievel
44 Shirt type
45 Theater sign
46 Miss Fabray, to friends
47 Film star Everett and namesakes
49 Reside
53 British essayist
55 Numero ___
57 Goddess, in Caesar's time
58 Famous comedienne
62 Closes tightly
65 Needy
66 Johnson
67 Shoe part
68 Goes astray
69 Musical piece
70 Mystery writer Masterson et al.
71 Hawaiian goose
72 Sea eagle

DOWN

1 Namesakes of writer Rogers St. Johns
2 Lab utensil
3 Nastier
4 Common contraction
5 Cared
6 Other
7 Prognosticator
8 Like some rocks
9 Sun disks
10 Grand Central, for one: Abbr.
11 Indian weight
12 Vetch
14 1051
21 Savory jelly
22 Boxwoods, e.g.
26 Place for cash
27 Mauna ___
28 Remnant
30 Hebrew month
32 Gave the once-over
33 Unit
36 Vacillate
38 Kind of worm
39 Unaspirated consonant
40 Meadowland
41 Zeal
42 Letters
43 Large tub
47 Jewelry parts
48 Bribe
50 Channel-swimmer Gertrude
51 Missive
52 Sail
54 Brilliance
56 Nightingale or Cavell
59 Shop sign
60 Knowledge
61 Xanthippe, for one
62 Vane letters
63 Old English letter
64 Well-known Greek nickname

ANSWER, PAGE 59

41

Themeless

ACROSS

1 Outer ___
6 Bullfighter's red cloak: Spanish
10 Discharge violently
14 Punctuation mark
15 Heroic poems
16 Cab
17 Audible
18 The graveyard shift
20 Lager
21 Devour
22 Small fish
23 Ripped
25 Astronomer Harlow ___
27 The Hun
30 Opposed: Colloq.
31 Baited
32 Dinnerware
33 Game official, for short
36 Distant
37 Fern leaf
38 Immature insect stage
39 Membranous pouch
40 Bake meat
41 Fixes potatoes
42 Newspaper name
44 Thomas à ___
45 Phantoms
47 Strong wind
48 Port and sherry
49 Sauté
50 Atop
54 Color named for TR's daughter
57 Fragrance
58 Flesh
59 Leeds's river
60 Summarize
61 March date
62 Musical pause
63 Worship

DOWN

1 Nature's protection for a cut
2 Telephone ___
3 Drug-producing plant
4 Baldassare's "The ___"
5 Finish
6 Arthur ___ Doyle
7 Entrance
8 Wooden pin
9 Residue from burning
10 Puts at a loss
11 Utility vehicle
12 Banishment
13 Clever
19 Lake source of the Blue Nile: Var.
21 Period
24 Elderly
25 Holy person
26 Female of the red deer
27 Expression of dismay
28 Porous limestone
29 Tragedy by Sophocles
30 Phantom
32 Lacking sensitivity
34 Fencing sword
35 Abstain from eating
37 ___ Knox
38 Portrayed
40 Lift
41 Thing: Law
43 Raises
44 Purchase
45 Hindu mystic
46 Stacked
47 Welcome
49 Mink and sable
51 Little, to Luigi
52 "___ Khayyám"
53 Back of the neck
55 Saloon
56 Prevaricate
57 ___ Parseghian

ANSWER, PAGE 61

42

Literary Flora

ACROSS

1 ___ California
5 Eugene V. ___
9 ___ Raton, Florida
13 S-shaped curve
14 A Fitzgerald
15 Dwell on, with delight
16 Sherwood play, with "The"
19 Corrida sound
20 Boston and San Francisco, e.g.
21 Mantric words
24 Race parts
26 Pelagic fisher
27 Keyboard instrument
29 ___ Angelico
30 Collection of reminiscences
33 Normandy city
34 Instruct
36 Romaine
37 Kipling work
41 Table part
42 "... ___ where the buffalo roam ..."
43 Peak
44 Before quattro
45 Fem. title
46 Qum native
49 GI address
50 Understood
51 Pismire
52 Alienate
56 ___-Magnon
58 Bromfield novel
63 Fortunetelling card
64 Hebrew letter
65 "Our ___": Wilder
66 Discharge
67 Anger
68 Had debts

DOWN

1 Jazz style
2 Ripen
3 Word with set or lag
4 Gas: Prefix
5 Conquer
6 Whitney or Wallach
7 Hallow
8 Notorious marquis
9 Double sirloin of beef
10 Finished
11 Price
12 Companion of crafts
15 Sutherland or Pons
17 Woes
18 "The ___ Queene": Spenser
21 Concealed
22 Not as nice
23 Kind of hammer
25 Quality which arouses pity
28 Wind dir.
29 Gradual appearance, on film
30 Legume yielding gum arabic
31 Lear or Mailer
32 Concur
35 Eyeball movement when dreaming: Abbr.
38 Bulwark
39 Royal seat
40 Son of Jacob
47 Fix a chair seat
48 Askew
49 Jargon
50 Where Nairobi is
52 Kitchen follower
53 Counterfeit
54 Actress Garr
55 Equipment
57 Preminger or Klemperer
59 "So ___": Ferber
60 Tier
61 Lamb's dam
62 Finale

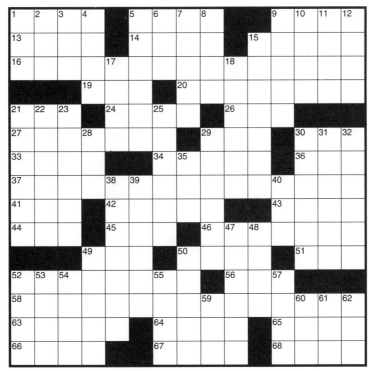

ANSWER, PAGE 63

43

Shoving Match

ACROSS

1 Christie and Hess, e.g.
6 Worms, at times
10 Sans date
14 Disconcert
15 Bombs and bullets, for short
16 Kelly's creature
17 Cattle catcher
18 Juices from spruces
19 Composer Khachaturian
20 "___ a Wonderful Life"
21 Bide one's time
23 Predicament
25 Office clerk
27 Brooks or Dekker
30 Canter
31 Lodz natives
32 Warms up
34 Rove
37 Harrow's rival
38 Claims
39 Gambler's game
40 Orly arr.
41 Elder statesman, in Japan
42 Bean or horse
43 Couple
44 Park employee
45 Pants of a sort
50 Uniformly
51 Bridge position
52 "___ Maria"
55 Shankar of the sitar
56 Breaks bread
58 Stair post
60 Sedgwick or Adams
61 Came down
62 Calliope's sister
63 Bear's order
64 Actor Auberjonois
65 Synthetic fiber

DOWN

1 Spanish surrealist
2 Blind as ___
3 "___ Appeal": Lemmon movie
4 Double curve
5 April phenomena
6 Fundamental
7 Cremona craftsman
8 Mischief-maker
9 Drunkards
10 Meager
11 Pentateuch
12 Wide open
13 TV's Pyle
22 Formicary denizen
24 Chalices
25 Hammer part
26 Gaucho's ground
27 Mimics
28 Large amount
29 Rorschach item
32 Indian native
33 Ending for auction or mountain
34 Crew
35 Funnyman Johnson
36 Cupboard feature
38 1988, for one
39 Dolphin organs
41 Dupe
42 Law firm member
43 Doctorow's "The Book of ___"
44 Legal thing
45 Israel's Shimon
46 Sidestep
47 Printer's apprentice
48 Take hold
49 Celerity
52 Absent
53 Presidential prerogative
54 North Carolina college
57 Toby's contents
59 Historic time

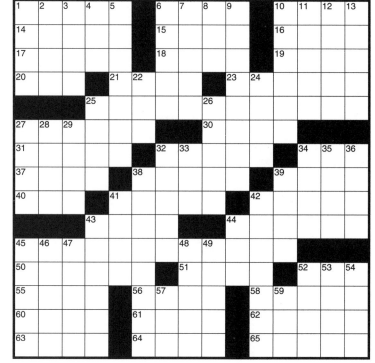

ANSWER, PAGE 57

44

Animal Crackers

ACROSS

1 Bric-a-___
5 Pinnacle
9 Young bull
13 Returnee's need, briefly
15 Do in
16 Kind of code
17 Related on mom's side
18 Fish's prime time?
20 Snuggle up
22 Hawaiian volcano goddess
23 Between due and quattro
24 "Gadzooks!"
26 Use up, as energy
28 Go on
31 Words to Brute
32 Flooring, in Faversham
33 Partner of 60-Down
35 Weasel's kin
39 Boris Becker often
40 It's sometimes tossed
42 Clerical calendar
43 Part of TGIF
45 Abie's girl
46 Want
47 Oklahoma city
49 Thespians, frequently
51 Non-productive
54 Lover's promise
55 Pierre's pal
56 Distant
58 Jewish month
62 Ferdinand snoozes?
65 Suburb near Minneapolis
66 On the Aegean
67 Talk wildly
68 Copter feature
69 Cherry and ruby
70 Capp of comics
71 Well-bred chap

DOWN

1 British gun
2 M. Descartes
3 Exclamations of discovery
4 Gossipy location?
5 Horned viper
6 Trims the hedge
7 Manufac-turer's brand
8 Hole in one's shoe
9 Head covering
10 Wife of Alcinous
11 Acquire knowledge
12 Was duplicitous
14 Contradict
19 Page size, formerly
21 Flexible blades
25 Painter Munch
27 Tease one's pet?
28 Realtor's map
29 Very sweet, as a dessert
30 Draft classification
31 Item that expunges
34 Top musical group of the 1970s
36 Corner
37 Kassel's river
38 Gangsters' guns
41 Sample recordings, for short
44 Do a baker's job
48 "___ penny, in ..."
50 Else
51 Children's storied pachyderm
52 Entertain
53 Irritated
54 Leaning
57 Muslim call to prayer
59 Pungency
60 Partner of 33-Across
61 Dessert
63 Vegas lead-in
64 Pen

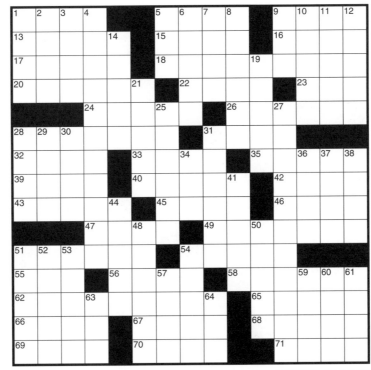

ANSWER, PAGE 59

45

Marketline

ACROSS

1 Where the action is in wheat or pork bellies
5 "___ should have a good memory"
10 Muscat is its capital
14 "Able was I ___ saw ..."
15 Wilkes-___, PA
16 Candy item
17 Former executive's plum, in case of 55-Across
20 These prompt a "gesundheit"
21 Buy or sell, to a broker
22 Trevi Fountain contents
23 Farm unit
25 Sun god
28 Breakfast item
29 Flat fish
32 Chairman Greenspan of the Federal Reserve
33 Ex Attorney General
34 Compass dir.

35 Cash cows, at times
39 French season
40 Vieux ___, New Orleans area
41 Garfield's pal
42 "___ Rosen-kavalier"
43 Authority on roast pig
44 Drop a stock from the Amex
46 Skirt feature
47 Related
48 A basic industry
51 Titanic's undoing
55 Raider's success

59 Stop sign, in Saltillo
60 ___ Haute, IN
61 Maui bird
62 College bigwig
63 Fear
64 Certain race

DOWN

1 Holds prices at a level
2 Something to pump
3 Vision beginning
4 Moonlighter's business
5 Doubleday and Yokum
6 Interruption

7 Tax-deferred plan, for short
8 Airport abbr.
9 Farm power agcy.
10 Earthy pigment
11 Whittier's "___ Muller"
12 Pay up
13 ___-do-well
18 Basso Pinza
19 What the Hunts tried in silver
23 Rocky ridge
24 ___ Grande, AZ
25 Abhorred
26 Thrill
27 Basketball pro from LA

28 "It ain't over till it's over" originator
29 "___ Do"; 1926 Hirsch-Rose song
30 Nay sayers
31 Harass
33 Scout badge
36 Spots on a peacock feather
37 Arab provincial governor
38 Rare note backed by a commodity
44 Tied up at the marina
45 "Waiting for the Robert ___"
46 ___ Hall University
47 Coronet
48 Food fish
49 Decorated tinware
50 "Cómo ___ usted?"
52 Always
53 California rockfish
54 Gold diver Louganis
56 Brit. company designation
57 Addendum for auction
58 Uno, due, ___

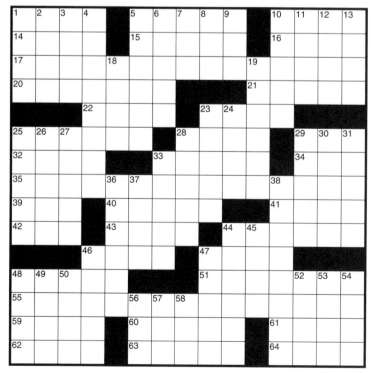

ANSWER, PAGE 61

46

Mr. President

ACROSS
1 Skyline element
6 Hole-punchers
10 Observation
14 "Our Miss Brooks" star
15 Photo
16 Demonic
17 Appoint an associate
18 White House nickname
20 Spend big
22 Severe
23 Tourney respite
24 Rugged cross
25 Nosh
26 Twofold
29 Vesper
32 Voluntary
34 Intensify
38 Family female
39 Gunpowder, e.g.
41 Uncle Tom's creator
42 Diamond thefts
44 Hulk Hogan, e.g.
46 Lads
48 Grid unit
49 Junior
52 Invalid
53 Ending with Michael
55 Personal view
57 English poet
61 Scottish waterway
63 TV component
64 On a par with
65 Nuremberg numeral
66 Reykjavik money
67 Whiplash reminder
68 Snicker ___
69 Heron's cousin

DOWN
1 Bursae
2 Bolster
3 Baalim figure
4 Major party
5 Journal record
6 Tennis great
7 Fictional first baseman
8 "Martin Eden" author
9 Banned Olympic drug
10 NBA five
11 Like Humpty Dumpty
12 Leg bone
13 Privileged group
19 Dolor
21 Turned right
24 Took up again
26 Insistent demands
27 Gram or dram
28 Bonnet inhabitant
30 Old hand
31 Famous address
33 Come through
35 Actress Negri
36 Aquarian tote
37 Kin to a wimp
40 Part of ETA
43 Mates
45 Salinger girl
47 Dessert apple
49 Phillips, e.g.
50 Antipasto item
51 Mailer's forte
54 Wide-eyed
56 Made go
57 Wall St. institution
58 Scent
59 The odds
60 Just so
62 Chemical ending

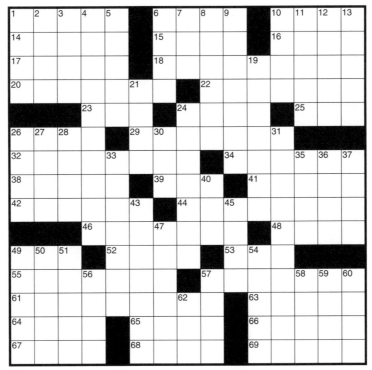

ANSWER, PAGE 63

47
Optical

ACROSS
1 Beaten, in chess
6 Con game
10 Crew
14 Got up
15 Storyteller's source
16 It's the duck in "Peter and the Wolf"
17 Ages
18 "___ go bragh"
19 Getting ___ years
20 Flirt
22 Adventure
23 Actress Moreno
24 Dotes on
26 Levanter
30 Ice house
32 Bard's river
33 Northern constellation

35 Bank, in New Orleans
39 Case establishing rights for suspects
41 Contradicting
43 Run off
44 St. Paul's architect Sir Christopher
46 Within: Prefix
47 A Castle
49 Haunt
51 Apollo, for one
54 Alençon
56 Acapulco aunties
57 Shrewd watchfulness

63 Poker term
64 Certain sax
65 Commun. device
66 Collar insert
67 Rod's partner
68 Stocking thread
69 Patriot Nathan
70 Florida's Miami-___ County
71 Henry James' biographer et al.

DOWN
1 Thank-you-___
2 Certain code
3 Seized

4 Slave of old
5 Mojave
6 Frozen rain
7 Pirate
8 Solo performance
9 Intellectual
10 Flirter's look
11 Capp character
12 Din
13 Men, for short
21 Ramp sign
25 Plaything
26 Ditto
27 Cleric's topic
28 Italy's Aldo
29 "Nonsense!"
31 Comic Kaplan
34 Sign of ennui

36 Hollywood intersector
37 Remnants
38 Very personal matters
40 Fictional Wolfe
42 ___ Pratt, famed name in Baltimore
45 Akin
48 Playwright Albee
50 Pvt. Bailey of the comics
51 Store
52 Utah mountain range
53 About birth
55 Cornmeal
58 Where Zeno held sway
59 Wallace or Ogden
60 Threat word
61 Cheerleader's routine
62 Former spouses

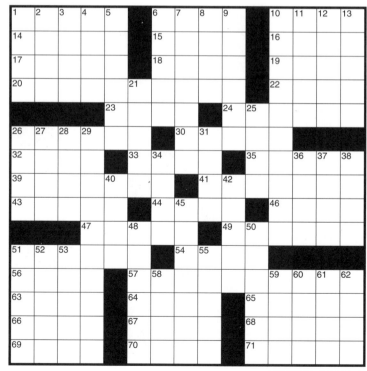

ANSWER, PAGE 57

52

48
Timely Names

ACROSS

1 Bends in a mountain road
6 Scottish laird
11 Noisy session
14 "The March King"
15 "... quoth the ___ ..."
16 One, to Jacques
17 "Pretty Poison" star
19 Show agreement
20 Be winning
21 Poet and author follower
22 Nota ___
23 Genie Barbara
24 Old age: Archaic
26 Tropical fish
28 Former servant
30 Swimming
33 Moon runabout
36 News ___
38 British fodder
39 Make use of
41 Shove
43 Winter month, in Seville
44 Hosts
46 Goddess of fate
48 Go bad
49 As of yesterday
50 Cats and dogs, e.g.
52 Dislike intensely
53 Poetic contraction
54 Binder
58 Encouraging sounds
60 Harrison
62 Was ubiquitous
64 Actress Rehan
65 Film star of yore
67 Country in Eur.
68 ___ Park, NJ
69 Pierre's income
70 Comp. bearing
71 Piqued
72 Mystery novel award

DOWN

1 Name in cosmetics
2 Puget of Washington State
3 Glove material
4 Member of a monastic brotherhood
5 Actress Thompson
6 Rugger score
7 Hemmed and ___
8 Birds: Latin
9 Wrestling holds
10 Material sale offering
11 Wife of Fred MacMurray
12 Later
13 Persian's companion
18 Contraction
22 Orchestra-leader's utensil
25 Ogle
27 Obvious
29 "___ Night"
31 Royal fiddler
32 Part of a dressage competition
33 Bert of "The Wizard of Oz"
34 Bacchanalian cry
35 "Alice in Wonderland" character
37 One of a crew
40 Starts of inventions
42 Be gloomy
45 More inflexible
47 Fashion's Oscar de la ___
51 Like some prunes
53 Glorify
55 In the midst of
56 Five: Prefix
57 Lawn implement
58 Fury
59 Former British protectorate
61 Sicilian resort
63 Jane of literature
65 Athos pal
66 A Stooge

ANSWER, PAGE 59

49

Racquet Squad

ACROSS

1 Heavenly body
5 Castle protector
9 British bus. abbreviation
12 Guthrie
13 Chat
14 Netman Becker
16 Top Grand Slam tournament site
18 Former Mrs. Trump
19 Part of ASAP
20 Played at the net
22 Japanese church
24 Actor Asther of old films
25 Family drs.
28 Netman Bjorn
30 Reducer
34 Item that's sometimes bum
35 Historic times
37 Military landing place: French
38 Dry
40 Maison part
42 Pack
43 Kind of bath
45 Metal dross
46 Fruit quaff
47 Starts the match
49 African village
51 Clay-court hue
52 About
54 Plod
56 Dealing with short lobs
60 Like some architecture
64 Sans ___
65 Grand Slam tournament site
67 Pianist Rubinstein
68 Canadian native
69 Edges
70 Kind of spin
71 Vats
72 For fear that

DOWN

1 "I never ___ purple cow ..."
2 Baseball's Speaker
3 Charity
4 Automaton
5 Four-time US Open champ, and family
6 Naval off. in charge
7 Russian sea
8 Joint part
9 Won in ___: blanked the opponent
10 Common tennis award for a runner-up
11 Feast
14 ___ Jean King
15 Downcast
17 Leopold's partner in crime
21 Hat
23 Wall hanging
25 Fast court surface
26 Ex ___: one-sided
27 Snoop
29 Annoys
31 Turkic Crimean
32 Work by Horace
33 Marry again
36 Blind sections
39 Coveted world trophy
41 Deuce games, at the French Open
44 Monolith
48 ___ Lanka
50 Entrance
53 Pass, as a statute
55 Wood knot
56 FDR agcy.
57 Comedian Sahl
58 Stanley Steamer, for example
59 Indian teacher
61 Romanian court cut-up
62 Ambitions
63 Historic cartoonist
66 Japanese money

ANSWER, PAGE 61

50

No Stops

ACROSS
1 Whatever
5 Sky pilot
10 Boat a fish
14 Jacob's twin
15 Nary ___:
no one
16 43-Across
org.
17 With
56-Across,
January
observance
20 Sobriquet for
Maryland
21 Have-not
22 Get the nod
23 Take kids to
school
24 Phrase
associated
with the
observance
30 Despondent
33 Gas the car
34 Paintings
35 Kind of fine
china
36 "... ___ wind
that blows ..."
37 Bulls, Bullets,
etc.
38 Green
gemstone
39 Tucker out
40 Task
41 Declaimed at
length
42 Shoe width
43 Concern
associated
with the
observance
45 Actor
Selleck
46 Stock finish
47 Land of
sangria
50 Attention-
getting
56 See 17-Across
58 If not
59 Perfume
bottle
60 Reuner
61 Sambar
62 Peevish
63 Bedews

DOWN
1 Landsman of
yore
2 Client
3 Early
residence
4 Actor
Cronyn
5 Incomplete
6 Take ___:
resist
7 "Act!"
8 Mystic sign
9 Capital of
Luanda?
10 Portals
11 Aspirin's
target
12 Beat it
13 Spencer
Tracy film,
1936
18 To boot
19 Word on a
coin
23 Get one's
licks
24 Teed off
25 Ice queen of
yesteryear
26 Blazing
27 Contemptible
28 Shul VIP
29 Notable time
period
30 Averse
31 Beginning
32 Tends the
garden
35 Boast
37 Fall mo.
38 Clergyman
40 McKay or
Palmer
41 Neat
43 Gram.
abbreviation
44 Lasso
45 Detroit
ballplayer
47 Brief
timetable
48 Amassment
49 Faulkner hero
50 Wimbledon's
Arthur
51 Boxscore
entries: Abbr.
52 Unfreeze
53 On strike
54 Astro chaser
55 Sweat shops?
57 UPI dispatch

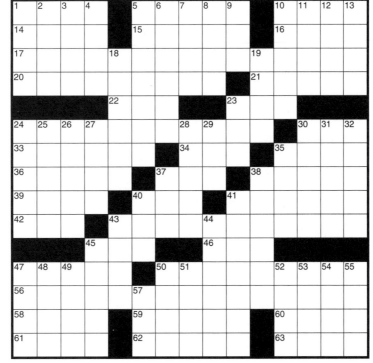

ANSWER, PAGE 63

1

```
S C O W L   B L A H     A I M
T A H O E   R E N E   U L N A
U P I N T H E A I R   P A N S
D E O   H A T   T O U R I S T
    D E S     A N N O
P E S O   S P A     P A G E
A L A W   L O N E   E R A S E
D O W N W E N T M C G I N T Y
S P E A R   D E M O   O G E E
  E R N E     S A P   U S E D
    D A D A     I N S
R E V O K E S   W E E   L A K
A L O U   U P S I D E D O W N
F L I T   C E E S   D I A N E
T A D     E N C E   S E N S E
```

6

```
A C E S   M A S S E   C O R M
G O A T   A F L A T   A R E A
O R S O   S O U T H E R N E R
O R T   A C O R   N E E D Y
D O E S N O T   E S T E
  B R A C T   E X T E R N A L
S O N N Y   S P E A R   O P A
T R E K   F A I R Y   D R A T
E E R   M U L C T   V O T R E
R E S T O R E S   M I G H T
    R O S S   R E D E E M S
T H A I S   M U S E   R E M
W E S T E R N E R S   O N N O
O R E O   H O R A E   L E T T
S E A N   O B O L S   E R S E
```

11

```
M O T O   S T A T E   Y A K S
E V E R   H I R A M   C L E O
N A T A T O R I U M   L E E S
O L E   A R E A   A T E M P O
    A C T S   S N I P
C R O C K S   P O U L T I C E
L O B E S   R E B E L   D A M
A M O S   H O T E L   R I S E
N E E   S O L E R   Q U O T E
G O S S A M E R   C U T T E R
    E R O S   T E E S
I N D I A N   O R A L   O W E
V O I D   Y U G O S L A V I A
A N N E   M N E M E   P E R T
N O E L   S E E P S   T R E S
```

15

```
S O D A S   S H A P E   A G E
A G E N T   E A R E D   L O N
P L A T O O N S E R G E A N T
S E R I O U S   S T E A M E R
    P I E S     T O R Y
R E M I S S   T O A D S
I V A N   G E N R E   G A S
F I R S T L I E U T E N A N T
E L K   R O L L S   A S T A
    E A G L E   R A T H E R
O N E R     D R A M
F O L L I E S   A V E R A G E
F I V E S T A R G E N E R A L
E S E   E N S U E   D E N I M
R E S   E A S E D   S L O T S
```

19

```
S L O T   R I T A S   J I B E
H I L O   U T I L E   I D O L
A M E N   S C R A P   N E A L
D O G I N T H E M A N G E R
    C A Y   O L E O
M O S S Y   G A S   H I R E D
I D I   S U R   U R S U L A
D O G D A Y S O F S U M M E R
A N N U L S   M I A   O C T
S T E N O   S A X   T A R T S
    G N A T   A I R
  S H A G G Y D O G S T O R Y
S O A R   A L I G N   I D E A
E L I E   T E R R E   S E A M
W O R E   E S T E S   T S P S
```

23

```
O T H E R   A S T O   C O D A
R O O N E   S H O P   O D I N
S L O O P   P A N E   N E A T
O D D L O T S H O R T S A L E
    A R E   W A R T
T S P   T A L C   S A R G E S
A T R I   S A L E   C I R C A
M A I N T E N A N C E C A L L
P R O V O   K I T E   T I A S
S T R E S S   M E A L   L T A
    N C O S   S I S
M O S T A C T I V E S T O C K
O L E O   C A N E   T O R A N
L I A R   E L O N   E R A S E
D O R Y   R E N T   R E L E E
```

27

	A	M	M	O		A	S	C	A	P		S	P	Y
S	W	E	A	R		N	O	I	R	E		W	O	E
C	A	T	S	A	N	D	D	O	G	S		E	O	N
O	R	A		T	O	R	A		U	T	T	E	R	S
W	E	L	C	O	M	E	S		M	E	A	T		
			A	R	E	A		M	E	R	G	E	R	S
M	U	L	T	I			P	I	N		N	I	P	
A	S	I		O	D	D	L	O	T	S		E	V	A
R	E	Q			R	A	Y			E	G	R	E	T
C	R	U	I	S	E	D		A	L	P	E			
		I	R	I	S		C	L	E	A	N	S	E	R
W	I	D	E	N	S		L	I	A	R		A	G	O
I	C	I		B	I	D	A	N	D	A	S	K	E	D
N	O	T		A	E	R	I	E		T	H	E	S	E
A	N	Y		D	R	U	M	S		E	A	S	T	

31

D	O	D	O		B	O	L	A	S		B	L	A	B
A	V	O	W		A	M	O	R	E		L	A	N	E
C	A	R	L	S	B	A	D	C	A	V	E	R	N	S
E	L	Y		H	I	R	E			A	N	D	E	S
			T	U	E	S		L	O	R	D			
B	A	G	E	L	S		S	E	L	L	E	R	S	
A	S	E	A			S	H	A	D	E		O	U	I
T	H	E	S	A	N	T	A	F	E	T	R	A	I	L
H	E	S		L	U	R	K	S			A	N	T	E
	N	E	C	K	T	I	E		C	U	R	S	E	S
			H	A	S	P		L	O	N	E			
S	T	E	A	L		W	A	I	T		P	A	S	
P	E	T	R	I	F	I	E	D	F	O	R	E	S	T
A	L	O	T		A	T	A	L	E		A	S	I	A
T	E	N	S		D	A	R	E	D		T	O	N	Y

35

B	E	L	G		A	B	A	S		T	R	I	T	E
E	R	I	E		R	A	C	E		E	A	T	E	N
A	G	O	N		I	N	C	A		A	S	S	E	S
D	O	N	A	L	D	J	T	R	U	M	P			
			I	L	O		R	E	S	T	S			
S	A	T	I	N	Y		E	N	I	D		E	P	H
A	S	I	D	E		F	L	E	A		A	R	L	O
T	H	E	A	R	T	O	F	T	H	E	D	E	A	L
E	I	R	E		A	C	I	S		L	O	T	T	E
S	E	C		A	K	I	N		O	B	S	E	S	S
		R	E	A	D	E			I	T	O			
			T	O	N	Y	S	C	H	W	A	R	T	Z
A	E	S	O	P		O	K	I	E		N	O	S	E
P	R	I	N	T		D	Y	E	R		O	M	A	R
E	S	T	E	S		H	E	R	S		N	E	R	O

39

M	U	L	C	T		W	A	F	T		B	I	B	S
E	N	E	R	O		E	L	L	A		A	D	I	T
A	S	T	O	P		A	L	U	M		R	I	S	E
			C	H	E	R	O	K	E	E	R	O	S	E
S	A	N		A	N	E	Y	E		T	I	M	E	R
Q	U	E	S	T	S			C	H	E	S	T	S	
S	T	A	T		I	L	O	I	L	O				
	O	R	A	N	G	E	B	L	O	S	S	O	M	
			I	N	D	I	E	S		A	R	E	A	
G	R	A	D	E	S			E	I	L	E	E	N	
R	E	L	I	C		A	B	E	T	S		S	K	Y
A	P	P	L	E	B	L	O	S	S	O	M			
C	O	I	L		A	L	I	T		P	E	O	N	Y
E	R	N	E		W	I	S	E		O	S	I	E	R
S	T	E	R		L	E	E	R		D	A	L	E	S

43

D	A	M	E	S		B	A	I	T		S	T	A	G
A	B	A	S	H		A	M	M	O		P	O	G	O
L	A	S	S	O		S	A	P	S		A	R	A	M
I	T	S		W	A	I	T		S	C	R	A	P	E
		P	E	N	C	I	L	P	U	S	H	E	R	
A	L	B	E	R	T		L	O	P	E				
P	O	L	E	S		H	E	A	T	S		G	A	D
E	T	O	N		L	I	E	N	S		F	A	R	O
S	S	T		G	E	N	R	O		P	I	N	T	O
			D	U	A	D		R	A	N	G	E	R	
P	E	D	A	L	P	U	S	H	E	R	S			
E	V	E	N	L	Y		E	A	S	T		A	V	E
R	A	V	I		E	A	T	S		N	E	W	E	L
E	D	I	E		A	L	I	T		E	R	A	T	O
S	E	L	L		R	E	N	E		R	A	Y	O	N

47

M	A	T	E	D		S	C	A	M		G	A	N	G
A	R	O	S	E		L	O	R	E		O	B	O	E
A	E	O	N	S		E	R	I	N		O	N	I	N
M	A	K	E	E	Y	E	S	A	T		G	E	S	T
				R	I	T	A		A	D	O	R	E	S
S	E	M	I	T	E		I	G	L	O	O			
A	V	O	N		L	Y	R	A		L	E	V	E	E
M	I	R	A	N	D	A		B	E	L	Y	I	N	G
E	L	O	P	E		W	R	E	N		E	N	D	O
			I	R	E	N	E		O	B	S	E	S	S
S	U	N	G	O	D		L	A	C	E				
T	I	A	S		W	E	A	T	H	E	R	E	Y	E
A	N	T	E		A	L	T	O		T	E	L	E	X
S	T	A	Y		R	E	E	L		L	I	S	L	E
H	A	L	E		D	A	D	E		E	D	E	L	S

2

```
WHAT  ■ CAPET ■ AGHA
AIDE  ■ ALULA ■ URAL
GRANDCANAL   ■ TARE
STREET ■ GNOMONIC
■ MEIN ■ NEED ■
TIGER ■ EVE ■ ADMIT
HORN ■ BEAMED ■ ODE
ANAT ■ EDUCE ■ SNEE
WIN ■ TELLER ■ EDAM
SADIE ■ ETE ■ GAELS
■ HOER ■ SLAW ■
WOODNOTE ■ ARREAR
ASTI ■ GRANDBANKS
THEN ■ EERIE ■ CCIV
TALE ■ RESTS ■ KEMP
```

7

```
IMPEL ■ ERSE ■ TESS
BAUME ■ GAIT ■ OATH
OLLIENORTH   ■ OSLO
■ IEIKA ■ EKE ■ TOE
SPA ■ ARDEB ■
EWE ■ AGO ■ INEPT
OVEN ■ LANA ■ SCREE
PESSIMISTICALLY
UNTIL ■ NETS ■ SILL
STILL ■ TIA ■ ENA
■ NESTS ■ CIA ■
LAD ■ END ■ ASSET
ELIA ■ SOUTHKOREA
AMEN ■ TREE ■ ELMAN
FAST ■ SETA ■ WEARY
```

12

```
HUGO ■ PERDU ■ HANG
OLES ■ ORION ■ EBEN
ONTHEPROWL ■ NITA
CATALPA ■ NEAREST
HEY ■ ALTS ■ AMY ■
■ SNEAKPREVIEW
SALAD ■ YENS ■ SPA
EVIL ■ PJS ■ PAID
REM ■ IDEA ■ LANCE
BRACKETCREEP ■
■ REF ■ KUDO ■ AMS
ADVISED ■ NINEVEH
LEAS ■ CRAWLSPACE
MANE ■ TELAE ■ ONCE
ALES ■ SWAYS ■ STAR
```

16

```
BARRE ■ CICS ■ SAGO
AVAIL ■ IRON ■ EDEN
SONIA ■ NASA ■ POLE
TWASTHENIGHT ■
EST ■ ISM ■ EERIE
■ NOTACREATURE
STEEN ■ RUST ■ MAR
ARMS ■ MOORE ■ MOTO
MAI ■ MASC ■ FARES
BYTHECHIMNEY ■
ASSAM ■ AES ■ LOY
■ WOULDBETHERE
ASIS ■ PORE ■ IONIA
LACE ■ ORAL ■ VEINS
AGER ■ NETS ■ ERNST
```

20

```
BARS ■ CHET ■ MONO
ALOP ■ PHAGE ■ AVON
TINA ■ LEHAR ■ CINE
STARTOFADECADE
■ SIT ■ STAR ■
MAJESTIC ■ ELOPES
ADO ■ EDIT ■ INUSE
JANUARYTHEFIRST
OMENS ■ LEAR ■ SEA
RESTON ■ STRIDENT
■ ANEW ■ ACE ■
NINETEENNINETY
BING ■ TAMED ■ TARO
ECOL ■ EVILS ■ EVER
GENE ■ DELL ■ DESK
```

24

```
LENS ■ WANT ■ CLEAT
IRAE ■ EMIR ■ RINSE
DISC ■ LOCI ■ EMOTE
■ CHARLIECHAPLIN
NUB ■ IST ■ ANY
BUSTERKEATON ■
ITO ■ DEAR ■ RASPY
DADA ■ DINER ■ BORE
SHARD ■ STAB ■ SOW
■ KEYSTONEKOPS
APT ■ SST ■ CSA
LAURELANDHARDY
OUTER ■ PARE ■ ARAB
FLOAT ■ LIAR ■ TALE
TARPS ■ ELMO ■ EYED
```

28

```
GAPE   PFC    TREE
ERIS   ROOF   HEAD
ANEST  IONA   EBRO
PUNCHANDJUDY
PATIENTS    SOEER
     SRI   STRATA
ITE    MIDI   ARNIE
DAVIDANDGOLIATH
ALENE  FEND     STS
  UNCLES     ELI
  STILE  CROONERS
    DARBYANDJOAN
TYNE   IRAN   GUSTY
LEON   EINE   ERIE
CATT   MOE    REND
```

32

```
BLAME  MINUS    ROW
RURAL  ABORIGINE
ARMED  MARINATED
TEA   TARA    BASS
   GAMES   COO
SLEWED   SCOURER
CADET  SHUNT   VET
ADDS   GEESE  RAVE
NEO  MARES   JANUS
  SNOOPER  GANGES
    UTE   SERGE
DORS    PILE   LOB
IMITATIVE   ALIBI
MOOSEHEAD   BISON
SOT  FERNS   ESTES
```

36

```
TABS   DUOMO   PLAN
HERA   ATRIP   ROLE
URAL   NURSE   ONUS
MIN   PARSONWEEMS
BEDOUIN    DIM
   YOND  FOOLSCAP
YAWPS   DIVOT   ONO
ELIS   EULER   FROG
LON   SNEER   GUNNY
LEERIEST   BLEW
    AFR   IRELAND
MOUNTVERNON   LIE
OWLS   ADANO   CLEF
LENO   TOTEM   RICE
EDAM   EMERY   USER
```

40

```
ARM    AMES   PASSE
DEEM   RILE   OTTER
ETAL   ENSE   REARS
LONIANDERSON
ARE   STE   HUSTLE
STREP  DOORS   ION
    LID  GNU  GLAD
   LUCILLEBALL
EVEL   TEE    SRO
NAN   CHADS  DWELL
STEELE   UNO   DEA
   CAROLBURNETT
SEALS   POOR   ARTE
STRAP   ERRS   GLEE
WHITS   NENE    ERN
```

44

```
BRAC   ACME   CALF
REHAB  SLAY   AREA
ENATE  PIKESPEAK
NESTLE  PELE   TRE
    YIPES  EXPEND
PROCEED   ETTU
LINO   EVER   OTTER
ACER   SALAD  ORDO
THANK  ROSE   NEED
   ENID  EMOTERS
BARREN   TROTH
AMI  AFAR  SHEBAT
BULLDOZES   EDINA
ASEA   RANT   ROTOR
REDS   ANDY   GENT
```

48

```
ESSES  THANE   JAM
SOUSA  RAVEN   UNE
TUESDAYWELD   NOD
ENDEAR  ESS   BENE
EDEN   ELD   OPAH
    ESNE   NATANT
LEM   ITEM  STOVER
AVAIL   RAM  ENERO
HORDES   NORN  ROT
RECENT    PETS
  HATE   EEN  TAPE
RAHS   REX   TEEMED
ADA  ANNAMAYWONG
GER  MENLO  RENTE
ENE  IRATE  EDGAR
```

3

```
ARKS   CAPS      ITSA
DINT   ALLIE     SHAW
ICER   NOUNS     MEGA
THEOFAUGUST      FAR
    NOD     SARDINE
  LOGGIAS    YANG
REF  GADIN    YAHOO
ANNS   NEMOS    STAR
STATS   SMOKE    ETE
   VETO    SKIVERS
CLARETS      PET
HER    THISFORHIRE
ATOP   ETHEL    IDES
RUNE   RIODE    CONS
OPEN   NESS     SLOE
```

8

```
MODEM   OLAF    RACK
OPINE   DATA    ETUI
VASES   OPERATORS
ELK  SAR    SLOPES
    DRUB  PAILS
  GROPE   ENDUSERS
CHIP   SCREED    LOT
HAVEN   HIS    ELEMI
ANE  ELIOTS    ICER
PASSWORD   LACTO
   CHOPS    ITER
OPERAS    DPT   OMB
DELETEKEY    ANNIE
DALE   NIKE    CEILS
STAN   SPED    HOCKS
```

13

```
HAIG    SOTO    IGET
ASTA   STOOP    TORE
HASTHEUPPERHAND
  PAEAN   SINUATE
    PGA     ETC
ITSOUTOFMYHANDS
PULSE   NENE    ORA
STET   DELED    AMEN
UTE    ATOM    TREAD
SITSONONESHANDS
    PMS     HAP
  OPENAIR   ITALO
FORCINGONESHAND
ALAI   TOTES    ONER
DAME   SRAS     SEAS
```

17

```
WISP    CAST    ASTER
ANTA    OLIO    VERNE
STAN    RASP    ETUDE
HOLDONESHORSES
  WEAVE   YALTA
      ARM   TESSERA
  MISLEAD     IYAR
HASH   DREAD    DECK
ALLA     SCENERY
MEEKEST    ERA
    ESSES    ISSEI
  BEATADEADHORSE
LADLE   INGE    FALA
ORDER   USER    ATAR
SNAGS   MESS    ROMP
```

21

```
CLANG   ACLU    QUAD
OATER   SOON    USMA
PINTO   SERB    ANON
ENO  USED    ESSAYS
   GNAT   HAHA
MALADY   CATARACT
ABASH   BASED    LEA
ROM   OREGANO    LAP
IMA   GENET   WHOSE
ABRIDGED   ABATED
   BAIT    KNOW
COVEYS   JINX    RHO
AMEX   TOOL    IVIED
RARE   ELAN    NOTRE
DRYS   REDS    GAZES
```

25

```
GLAD    POST    PICTS
RAJA    LINE    ASHOT
UNAL    ALEX    STELA
BARLEYYEAST    REC
   ARM   RNA    ARTY
NEWSMAN    IDLY
ERA   ITALO    EATEN
AMS   NEVADAN    RAY
TAHOE   ERECT    ERE
   INST    STUDENT
CANE   OHS    IRA
EGG   MOUNTVERNON
SOTTO   MIRE    WOVE
AROAR   IDOL    ISEE
RANGE   DENY    NERD
```

29

```
A T L A S   L A S S   R O B T
L O I R E   A R E A   A G E E
A M M A N   C L A N   D E L E
  B A R N E Y O L D F I E L D
    A A R   S A L A
L I S T   N O D   L A T E S T
O R A   C I D E R   M O V I E
R E T I R E D G E N E R A L S
I N A N E   S A T E D   D A T
S E N S O R   S E W   M E S A
    P L U S     E R A
A N C I E N T M A R I N E R
M O O R   N O O N   F U M E D
O N C E   E V A N   L A M I A
R O O D   R E N E   E L A N D
```

33

```
A R A B S   U N T O   H A H A
P A N I C   R O O F   A P E R
T H E S O U N D O F M U S I C
  S W O R N   S T E E L E R S
    N E S S   S R A
H O E S   E L I   S N A R L S
A N N   P E O N S   I D E A L
R E T U R N O F T H E J E D I
P A R S E   P E R E S   S E T
S L E E V E   R I A   T E N S
      I N A   A L A R
I N K W E L L S   T R O T S
G O N E W I T H T H E W I N D
E N I D   S E E R   A E D E S
T O T S   T R A Y   S L E E T
```

37

```
M O T H   A M I S S   R A N K
A L A I   D I N A H   I D E A
A G O G   H I G H A N D D R Y
M A S H I E   A I D A   S O O
    F A R O   B E C H
F I L A M E N T   D R I P S
E N O L   N E E R   E G R E T
E S A U   T A P E S   H E W S
L E T T S   T I L E   S E E K
    T H I N K   D I A M O N D S
    N A N A   C H I C
A R I   R E M O   O R I O L E
H I G H L A N D E R   E G A D
A L O E   D I E T S   T E L E
T E R M   S A R E E   Y E A N
```

41

```
S P A C E   C A P A   S P E W
C O L O N   O D E S   T A X I
A L O U D   N I G H T U N I T
B E E R   E A T   S M E L T
    T O R N   S H A P L E Y
A T T I L A   G A I N S T
L U R E D   C H I N A   R E F
A F A R   F R O N D   P U P A
S A C   R O A S T   R I C E S
    H E A R S T   B E C K E T
S P I R I T S   G U S T
W I N E S   F R Y   U P O N
A L I C E B L U E   A R O M A
M E A T   A I R E   R E C A P
I D E S   R E S T   A D O R E
```

45

```
P I T S   A L I A R   O M A N
E R E I   B A R R E   C A N E
G O L D E N P A R A C H U T E
S N E E Z E S   O R D E R
    L I R E   A C R E
H E L I O S   B R A N   D A B
A L A N   M E E S E   E N E
T A K E O V E R T A R G E T S
E T E   C A R R E   O D I E
D E R   E L I A   D E L I S T
    S L I T   T O L D
S T E E L   I C E B E R G
H O S T I L E T A K E O V E R
A L T O   T E R R E   N E N E
D E A N   D R E A D   D R A G
```

49

```
S T A R   M O A T   L T D
A R L O   C O Z E   B O R I S
W I M B L E D O N   I V A N A
A S S O O N   V O L L E Y E D
    T E R A   N I L S
G P S   B O R G   D I E T E R
R A P   E R A S   E T A P E
A R I D   S A L L E   S T O W
S T E A M   S L A G   A D E
S E R V E S   S T A D   R E D
      I N R E   S L O G
S M A S H I N G   I O N I A N
S O U C I   A U S T R A L I A
A R T U R   C R E E   R I M S
T O P   T U N S   L E S T
```

4

```
T O I L █ █ A H E M █ L E C H
U N D O █ C L A R A █ I L A Y
B Y E B Y E B L A C K B I R D
A X E █ A R E S █ K A R A T E
█ █ █ G M E N █ P I T A █ █
M A D R A S █ A R N E █ B A S
O N I O N █ A L I A █ K A N T
W E E W I L L I E W I N K I E
E A T S █ O L E S █ M E E S E
R R S █ A N O N █ S P A R E D
█ █ K N E W █ P A I D █ █
S P E A K S █ B A N S █ E L I
H A Z Y H O T A N D H U M I D
A G R A █ M O L D Y █ S I S I
W E A K █ E M M A █ █ C R A G
```

9

```
P A A R S █ S L E D █ A S K S
O N T A P █ P E A R █ P L I E
K I T T Y B I T T Y █ R A T E
E T A █ W A N █ C L O N E D
S A R A H S █ █ B E I N G █
█ █ █ J O K E F O L K █ G U M
B A B A █ A R U L E █ A S A
A D O R E █ S A L █ S A N E R
N O R █ C H I M E █ M G R S
E S E █ L O N E Z O N E █ █
█ D R A N G █ M I S T E D
D I L A T E █ S A C █ R Y E
A V O N █ S Q U A R E F A R E
M A R T █ T U T S █ S I D E D
E N D S █ Y E A H █ T R E S S
```

14

```
H A L S █ S P A R █ R A M S
A S E A █ B L A R E █ E X I T
T H E F I R E N E X T T I M E
S E R E N A D E █ █ R I S E R
█ █ █ G I S █ B R I E █ █
S C R E E N █ M O O S █ A R C
H A I R █ C O R O T █ T A L
O N C E I N A L I F E T I M E
R O E █ M O V E S █ A L I A
E N D █ O N E S █ T I T T E R
█ █ A G E S █ E E N █ █
S T O L E █ A M E R I C A N
H A V I N G A F I N E T I M E
O R A N █ E A R L Y █ E T E S
P A L E █ T R O Y █ M E S S
```

18

```
J A M B █ M E T S █ R B I S
O V A L █ S A M O A █ E O N S
R I G A █ T R I P P █ V A S T
Y A N K E E C L I P P E R █
█ N I E C E █ █ H U R D S █
█ █ S U L T A N O F S W A T
G A R █ S O D A █ F E A T S
R E E F █ T O T █ S L A G
A S P I C █ E L A M █ K N T
F O R D H A M F L A S H █ █
█ P I G I N █ █ R E E S E
█ M E C H A N I C A L M A N
T H A T █ O R O N O █ M O V E
L A N E █ L O R D S █ E T E S
C M D R █ T O D O █ T E S T
```

22

```
P A C A █ P L U M P █ R S V P
A V O N █ R O L E O █ O L E O
L I V E █ O V E R P O W E R S
O V E R S E E S █ O N E W A Y
█ █ R O A M █ O V E N █ █
L A T I N S █ O V E R A C T S
E T U D E █ B L U R █ S H O W
G A R █ █ A R I L S █ █ A R E
I L E S █ N O V E █ P O N C E
T E S T C A S E █ C A U G H T
█ █ R U L E █ H A T E █ █
P L E A S E █ O V E R C O M E
R E D I S C O V E R █ A V O W
A G I N █ T R E N T █ S E R E
M O T S █ S O R T S █ T R E S
```

26

```
A M A H █ B B C █ O N S E T
R E M O █ R E A L █ U N I T E
C A M B R I D G E █ T E T E S
A T O N E D █ E M I L █ E S T
█ █ O L E █ D O R A L █ █
A L I B I █ █ N E W B U R G
T I N █ C A M E I N █ A V O N
E N D O █ S A U C E █ R U G A
A G E R █ A R R E S T █ L E T
R O X B U R Y █ █ H E A R S
█ █ S N U F F █ T E D █ █
A T T █ A M O R █ A M I E N S
C A R I B █ R O C H E S T E R
T R I A L █ D E M O █ O T T O
S O M M E █ █ S S E █ N E S S
```

30

```
A H A R D ■ R A T E D ■ O H S
N A M E D ■ O S A G E ■ N A Y
T H Y N E I G H B O R ■ E I N
E A S E ■ T E E S ■ A D A G E
■ ■ ■ G A I T ■ I N O N ■ ■ ■
A S I A N S ■ D I A G N O S E
L I N D A ■ D I A N E ■ T E A
O N D E ■ B E R G S ■ T H I S
A G E ■ R I N G O ■ G H E N T
D E C R E A S E ■ S P I R E S
■ ■ ■ E O N S ■ D I O R ■ ■ ■
A I M E E ■ S T A G ■ T E R I
R O B ■ W I T H T H E E Y E S
A T E ■ A W A R E ■ V E R D I
B A R ■ L O T U S ■ A N E S T
```

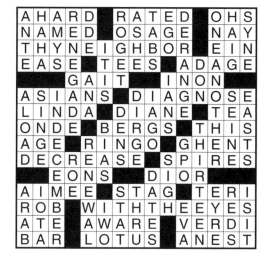

34

```
P A R ■ A B E D ■ O M A N
E L I A ■ L A R U E ■ T U L A
S T O C K I N D E X ■ I T E S
T A T T E D ■ A L T H O U G H
■ ■ ■ U R A L ■ S O U S A ■ ■
R E G A R D E D ■ R E E L E D
A M I T Y ■ H A S T Y ■ F R I
M E N E ■ T A R E S ■ H U A C
B E N ■ E R R E D ■ M A N S E
O R I A N A ■ R E M I N D E D
■ ■ E L O P E ■ R I N G ■ ■ ■
S A M P L E R S ■ N E S S I E
A L A I ■ Z E R O C O U P O N
A D E N ■ E C O L E ■ P A L I
R O S E ■ T S A R ■ T A D
```

38

```
B A M A ■ P O L A R ■ B R A S
A J A R ■ L U I S E ■ R O T A
S A N F R A N C I S C O B A Y
E X O ■ O N C E ■ ■ O W E N S
■ ■ ■ P A T E ■ A B A S ■ ■ ■
M O T O R S ■ T U R R E T S
A N I L ■ I O T A S ■ R A E
Y E L L O W S T O N E P A R K
A N D ■ R I L E S ■ E D G E
■ D E C A D E S ■ S C R E E D
■ ■ U T E S ■ T A L K ■ ■ ■
S M O T E ■ A R T E ■ F E E
W A L T D I S N E Y W O R L D
I D L E ■ T A T E R ■ L E A D
G E A R ■ S W I S S ■ D E N Y
```

42

```
B A J A ■ D E B S ■ B O C A
O G E E ■ E L L A ■ S A V O R
P E T R I F I E D F O R E S T
■ ■ ■ O L E ■ S E A P O R T S
O M S ■ L A P S ■ E R N ■ ■ ■
C E L E S T A ■ F R A ■ A N A
C A E N ■ T R A I N ■ C O S
U N D E R T H E D E O D A R S
L E G ■ A H O M E ■ A C M E
T R E ■ M R S ■ I R A N I A N
■ ■ A P O ■ K N E W ■ A N T
E S T R A N G E ■ C R O ■ ■
T H E G R E E N B A Y T R E E
T A R O T ■ A Y I N ■ T O W N
E M I T ■ R A G E ■ O W E D
```

46

```
S P I R E ■ A W L S ■ N O T E
A R D E N ■ S H O T ■ E V I L
C O O P T ■ H O N E S T A B E
S P L U R G E ■ D R A S T I C
■ ■ ■ B Y E ■ R O O D ■ E A T
D U A L ■ E V E N I N G ■ ■
U N B I D D E N ■ D E E P E N
N I E C E ■ T E A ■ S T O W E
S T E A L S ■ W R E S T L E R
■ ■ N I P P E R S ■ Y A R D
S O N ■ V O I D ■ M A S ■ ■
C L O S E U P ■ N E W B O L T
R I V E R S P E Y ■ A U D I O
E V E N ■ E I N S ■ K R O N A
W E L T ■ S N E E ■ E G R E T
```

50

```
S U C H ■ P A D R E ■ G A F F
E S A U ■ A S O U L ■ A C L U
R E V M A R T I N L U T H E R
F R E E S T A T E ■ N E E D Y
■ ■ ■ W I N ■ ■ B U S ■ ■ ■
I H A V E A D R E A M ■ L O W
R E F I L L ■ A R T ■ B O N E
A N I L L ■ N B A ■ P R A S E
T I R E ■ J O B ■ O R A T E D
E E E ■ C I V I L R I G H T S
■ ■ ■ T O M ■ A D E ■ ■ ■
S P A I N ■ A R R E S T I N G
K I N G J R S B I R T H D A Y
E L S E ■ P H I A L ■ A L U M
D E E R ■ T E S T Y ■ W E T S
```